THE SKEPTIC'S GUIDE™
to
Global Poverty

Tough Questions
Direct Answers

Dale Hanson Bourke

Authentic

COLORADO SPRINGS · LONDON · HYDERABAD

Authentic Publishing
We welcome your questions and comments.

USA   1820 Jet Stream Drive, Colorado Springs, CO 80921
       www.authenticbooks.com or 1-866-732-6657
UK   9 Holdom Avenue, Bletchley, Milton Keynes, Bucks,
       MK1 1QR, UK www.authenticmedia.co.uk
India Logos Bhavan, Medchal Road, Jeedimetla Village,
       Secunderabad 500 055, A.P.

The Skeptic's Guide^{TM} to Global Poverty

ISBN-13: 978-1932805-57-4
ISBN-10: 1-932805-57-5

Copyright © 2007 by Dale Hanson Bourke

10 09 08 07 / 6 5 4 3 2 1

Published in association with the literary agency of Alive Communication
Inc., 7680 Goddard Street #200, Colorado Springs, CO 80920.

Cover design: Paul Lewis
Interior design: Angela Lewis

Printed in the United States of America

Contents

About the Author

Dale Hanson Bourke is a consultant to nonprofit organizations and a columnist for *The Washington Post*. The author of eight books, she has served as editor and publisher of several magazines, and has traveled extensively in developing countries.

She has also served on the board of directors of World Vision US and International, International Justice Mission, and currently serves on the board of Opportunity International. She is the founder of the AIDS Orphan Bracelet Project.

The mother of two sons, she lives with her husband near Washington, DC.

Also by the author:
The Skeptic's Guide™ to the Global AIDS Crisis.

How much do you know about Global Poverty?

Test your knowledge with these true/false statements (answers on following page).

1. There has been little progress made in reducing global poverty in the last decade.

2. The US gives more money per capita to help alleviate poverty than any other nation.

3. Overpopulation is part of why sub-Saharan Africa is so poor.

4. Malaria kills more children in Africa than any other disease.

5. Obesity threatens the life expectancy of some developed countries.

6. The main job of the United Nations is to help the poor of the world.

7. The poorest people in the world are most likely to become terrorists.

8. Prostitution is illegal in most of the world.

9. Child labor is mostly found in sweatshops.

10. Illegal immigration is having a negative effect on the US economy.

A Quiz Answers

1. FALSE. Over the past decade, much progress has been made on many fronts to reduce poverty, improve living conditions of the poor, and help increase health and education.

2. FALSE. While the US gives the most amount of money overall, it does not rank in the top 20 in per-capita giving to the poor. (See page 17.)

3. FALSE. Sub-Saharan Africa is not densely populated except in a few major cities.

4. TRUE. Approximately 3,000 children die each day from malaria. (See page 54.)

5. TRUE. More than 300 million people worldwide suffer from obesity and related health conditions.

6. FALSE. It was originally founded to prevent future wars and still exists primarily to facilitate cooperation among countries in a variety of areas. (See page 73.)

7. FALSE. Most of the poorest of the poor lack the energy or resources to do much more than survive daily life. Terrorism tends to come from lower or middle class unrest. (See page 66.)

8. FALSE. Prostitution is actually legal in a number of countries and is not actually illegal in some (such as England) although solicitation is. (See page 69.)

9. FALSE. According to UNICEF, most children work in agriculture, sell products on the street, or are employed as domestic workers. (See page 68.)

10. TRUE and FALSE. Overall, the US needs more workers and people coming to the US illegally tend to fill jobs in agriculture and other areas. But pockets of the US economy are hurt because of US workers losing their jobs to labor willing to work at a lower cost. (See page 63.)

Acknowledgements

This book grows out of the many questions I received after people read *The Skeptic's Guide™ to the Global AIDS Crisis.* So I want to thank all of those people who took the time to read and respond to that book.

Thanks also to: Lynne Hybels who first suggested this book and encouraged me along the way; Ed Scott, who helped me shape these concepts, and whose commitment to educating the "rich" about the "poor" inspires many; Nancy Birdsall, president of Center for Global Development, who was generous with her time and insights; Makonen Getu, shepherd and scholar, whose personal and academic understanding of poverty sharpened the focus; and, friends at Opportunity International and World Vision who have educated me over the years about the causes of poverty.

Forming these concepts into a simple book was only possible through the help of: Rick Christian, my agent whose worldview, like mine, has been turned upside down by seeing poverty up close; Volney James, who has supported the concept of these books from the beginning; Angela Lewis, whose expertise, patience, creativity, and passion have made her more of a collaborator than editor; Tyler Bourke, photographer, computer expert, and counselor, who helped me in a variety of tasks; and, Chase and Tom Bourke, who are ever-patient and calm through the ups and downs of the editorial process.

Finally, I am humbled by the many people who are actively and often sacrificially involved in the cause of fighting poverty and advocating for the poor.

When drought hits southern Kenya, Faith and
her sisters often go without meals.

INTRODUCTION

If you are reading this book, you are probably not poor. You may feel poor compared to your friends and neighbors, but in the perspective of the world, you are not poor.

It is not just that the relatively modest cost of this book would exceed a poor person's income for a week; it is that the poor lack access to information. They do not have bookstores or libraries. Most cannot read. Those who go to school often leave at an early age to help support the family. And many suffer from impaired vision because they lack simple nutrients in their diets or suffer a small infection that goes untreated.

Being poor, it turns out, is much more complicated than lack of money. Poverty runs deep into the family and community, robbing individuals and whole societies of life-saving information, health care, food, and water. Poverty robs individuals not only of security and health, but also dignity. A poor person is often too busy surviving the present to spend much time thinking about the future. And yet, the poor do have dreams. *Voices of the Poor*, a series of books created by the World Bank, quotes poor people whose hopes and dreams—especially for their children—are much like ours.

Fixing poverty isn't easy either. So many have tried in so many ways that the average person views poverty as an intractable condition. Some even like to quote the words of Jesus, "You will always have the poor among you . . .", as evidence that poverty is simply part of the human condition.

But just as knowledge is power to the poor, it is also power to those of us who are relatively rich. We can make a difference, but we have to understand more. We need to be smarter about poverty.

This book is very basic. It is not written by or for economists or sophisticated relief and development specialists. It is written by an average person to help other average people understand what we all need to know about poverty. It attempts to explain basic principles, common causes, and sometimes confusing phrases and initials. It assumes a primarily American audience, simply because it is the place in the world where I stand.

There is a great divide in the world between the rich and the poor. But there is also a divide between the experts and the average citizens. While experts debate best practices, most of us lack understanding of the issues. This book attempts to offer a framework for understanding poverty.

Can we conquer poverty? Yes and no. We can help individuals and groups find their way out of poverty, although development experts emphasize that the process must be collaborative.

But the bigger picture is more challenging. How much are those of us who are relatively rich willing to sacrifice to help those who are extremely poor? How unselfish can we really be as societies? Are we willing to be less rich and perhaps less powerful in order to help people we don't know become less poor and less powerless?

Poverty is not only an economic problem, but also a cultural and spiritual challenge. It takes not just money to defeat poverty, it takes moral will and personal sacrifice.

If you are reading this book, you are one of the people in the world who can make a difference. It is up to you whether you accept that fact as a responsibility and embrace it as a challenge.

Acronyms

AIDS	Acquired Immune Deficiency Syndrome
CDC	Centers for Disease Control
EITC	Earned Income Tax Credit
EU	European Union
FBO	Faith-Based Organization
GAVI	Global Alliance for Vaccines and Immunization
GDP	Gross Domestic Product
HDI	Human Development Index
HHS	Deptartment of Health and Human Services
HIV	Human Immunodeficiency Virus
IDP	Internally Displaced Persons
IMF	International Monetary Fund
ILO	International Labor Organization
ITN	Insecticide Treated Nets
MCC	Millennium Challenge Corporation
MDG	Millennium Development Goals
NAFTA	North American Free Trade Agreement
NGO	Non Governmental Organization
ODA	Official Development Assistance
PEPFAR	President's Emergency Plan for AIDS Relief
PPP	Purchasing Power Parity
PVO	Private Voluntary Organization
TANF	Temporary Assistance for Needy Families
TB	Tuberculosis
UN	United Nations
UNAIDS	United Nations Program on HIV/AIDS
UNICEF	United Nations Children's Fund
UNDP	United Nations Development Program
USAID	United States Agency for International Development
WFP	World Food Program
WHO	World Health Organization

Poverty contributes to poor health and poor health contributes to poverty.

1 THE BASICS

Why do you think people are poor? is a question I have asked friends and strangers for the last several months. The discussions have sometimes been lively and sometimes ended quickly. Many people have strong feelings about poverty and why it exists. They have even stronger feelings about why people are poor and who the poor really are. But the basic facts often belie the assumptions. And people are sometimes afraid to ask those questions that seem politically incorrect. Certain questions seem to come up most often. They are listed below.

What does it mean to be poor? Is there an objective measure of poverty?

■ More than 1 billion people in the world live on less than $1 per day according to the World Bank. These people are considered the poorest of the poor and lack enough resources for basic survival. Worldwide, 2.7 billion live on less than $2 per day. Practically, that means that they are often hungry and malnourished, have limited or no access to clean water, no health care, and little or no access to education. The infant mortality rate is high, the life expectancy is low, and exposure to disease is constant and often deadly.

What's so bad about being poor? Aren't some poor people happier than those who are rich?

■ People who are poor often have a greater understanding of the value of life, the importance of family, and are grateful for basic necessities. Materialism has less chance of blurring their vision or cluttering

FACT:

Nearly half of the people in the world live on less than $2 a day.

their values, although they often wonder why others have so much when they have so little. The daily heartaches of the poor cannot be underestimated. Many mothers in poor countries have lost one or more of their children because of preventable disease, poor nutrition, or unsafe drinking water. Families cannot provide enough food for everyone so hunger is common. Women must give birth without medical help or proper sanitation and often die in childbirth. Living conditions are usually unsafe, and the poor are more likely to succumb to violence.

Jeffrey Sachs, author of *The End of Poverty*, distinguishes three degrees of poverty: extreme (or absolute), moderate, or relative. Extreme poverty occurs only in developing countries and means that "households cannot meet basic needs for survival."

Moderate poverty means "basic needs are met, but just barely." Relatively poor usually live in high-income countries but below the average national income or poverty line and "lack access to perquisites to upward mobility."

Aren't some poor people just lazy?

■ In general, poor people worker harder than anyone else. They don't have time-saving tools or appliances, must perform even simple tasks by hand, and lack easy access to food and water, so must often travel distances just to get basic necessities. They lack health insurance, so they must work even when they are ill, and they have no retirement or pension plan for old age. If a member of their family is ill, they must care for him or her in addition to the other work. Most poor people work long days without any "day off" or vacation.

“

The end of poverty will require a global network of cooperation among people who have never met and who do not necessarily trust each other.”

Jeffrey Sachs in The End of Poverty

Why do we hear so much about poverty in Africa? Aren't people poor in other parts of the world, too?

■ There are pockets of poverty in many parts of the world, but sub-Saharan Africa and South Asia have the greatest concentration of poverty. As a percentage of population, more people in Africa live on less than $1 per day than anywhere else in the world.

Latin America and the Caribbean also have a high concentration of poverty. When poverty is understood as not only lack of income, but also lack of health, education, and opportunities, the population of central and southern African countries suffers the most.

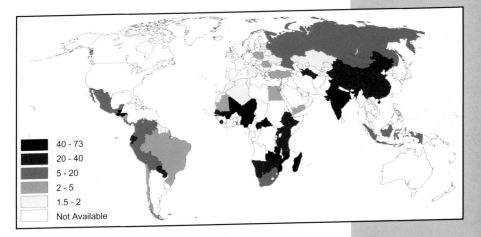

40 - 73
20 - 40
5 - 20
2 - 5
1.5 - 2
Not Available

Percent of the popluation living on less than US$1 per day at the beginning of 2000.

Why is a dollar a day the measure of poverty? Isn't it much less expensive to live in many countries?

■ There is no easy way to measure poverty across countries and cultures. Using the dollar as a measure is simply a way to translate the ability of a person to gain access to resources necessary to live. The equivalent of a dollar a day does not provide enough to secure basic nutrition, clean water, health care, or education.

Economists struggle to find an equitable way to compare poverty and wealth across countries. Most people look at their own income as a way to decide if they are relatively "rich" or "poor." But it is true that the cost of living varies even within regions of the same country. Currencies also fluctuate compared to one another.

Some standards attempt to adjust for differences across countries in prices and the cost of living. For example, a typical group of goods is often compared from country to country so that income in US dollars, for example, can be measured and compared using what is called the purchasing power parity (PPP) rate. One such measure was developed by *The Economist* using the price of hamburgers and is called the "Big Mac Index," but of course applies primarily to more developed countries.

Why is the US always asked to help other countries?

■ The US is a big nation and the richest in the world. The US economy is nearly three times the size of the next largest economy, and Americans along with some Europeans are personally wealthier than the citizens of almost all other countries. Because the US is so much wealthier and Americans have the

> "
> **If you can't feed a hundred people, then feed just one."**
>
> Mother Teresa

capacity to give, countries in need often see the US as their best hope.

Doesn't the **US** spend a huge amount of money on foreign aid?

■ In 2005, the US gave more than $27.5 billion in foreign aid, more than any other nation. But when you look at the amount of aid given as a percentage of the entire national budget, other countries are more generous. In fact, when measured this way, the US is not even in the top 20 countries in terms of generosity.

In addition, only a percentage of the foreign assistance budget goes to fighting poverty. Nearly 40 percent of the State Department's foreign aid budget goes to supporting strategic political allies like Israel, Pakistan, Egypt, and Jordan, and to fighting drugs.

Currently, the US gives .07 percent of its budget to foreign assistance. Along with other countries, the

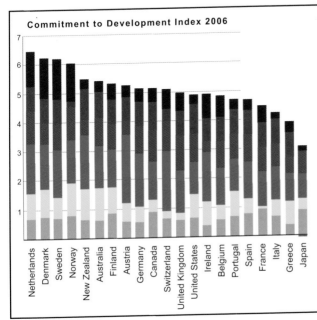

FACT:

The US economy is almost three times larger than Japan's, the next largest economy in the world.

The Commitment to Development Index ranks the richest countries on their dedication to policies that benefit the people living in the poorest nations.

Aid
Trade
Investment
Migration
Enviroment
Security
Technology

US has committed to give .7 percent of its GDP—10 times more than it currently does—so it is falling short compared to its commitment.

Why do most people think the US gives too much money to the poor overseas?

▪ When researchers ask Americans how much the US spends on foreign assistance, most people guess it is around 25 percent of the total budget. The average American thinks it should be reduced to 10 percent. Since the actual number is far less than 1 percent, there is a major disconnect between perception and reality.

Which nations give the most?

▪ While the US gives the highest amount of foreign aid, it does not give the highest percentage of its gross domestic product. In fact, the Nordic countries and the Netherlands are far more generous when measured in relative terms. That is why other countries sometimes criticize the US for not being generous enough.

How does the US government give money to the poor overseas?

▪ The US government gives money overseas through a number of different institutions. Its primary agency is USAID—the United States Agency for International Development—which partners with humanitarian organizations, local governments, schools and businesses to encourage the development of countries. During the Bush administration, two new institutions were created: the Millennium Challenge Corporation (MCC), which concentrates

> " Poverty is not about numbers. It is about inequality, and specifically about inequality in power relationships."
>
> Jayakumar Christian in *God of the Empty-Handed*

its aid on very poor but well governed countries, and PEPFAR, the President's Emergency Program for AIDS Relief. As many as three dozen other government agencies provide overseas development assistance (ODA) through grants, loans and commodities. In addition, the US supports a number of international organizations, including the Global Fund to Fight AIDS, TB, and Malaria, the World Bank, the International Monetary Fund, and the UN, all of which provide aid to the poor.

What is per capita income?

■ Per capita income takes the total income of a country and divides it by the population to arrive at an average. In a country like India, where the population is very large and the gap between rich and poor is great, the per capita income is quite low. In some industrialized countries with a smaller population, the per capita income is quite high.

What is the per capita income in the US? Is it the highest in the world?

■ According to the International Monetary Fund, per capita income in the US is just over $41,000. It is the third highest in the world, with Luxembourg at nearly $70,000 and Norway at more than $42,000.

© Dale Hanson Bourke

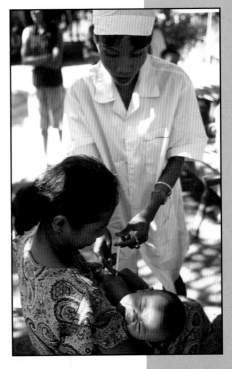

A government nurse immunizes a baby in Cambodia.

Why do so many charities ask for funds to help the poor if the government is already helping so much?

- The US government partners with many charities to provide on the ground assistance to the poor. Since many of the charitable organizations have staff in local communities, they are uniquely qualified to assess needs and then help ensure that the resources go to those in need.

When a charity receives a government grant, there is often an amount that must be matched through private funds in order to receive the money. This ensures that the mission of the organization is being supported by private donors and not just government monies.

In addition, the charity may work in specialized areas or do work that is not part of what the government supports. For example, activities that include a religious component cannot be supported by US government funds, although the general charitable work of faith-based organizations can. Giving to a charity is often a very direct way to help people in a specific community or with a particular need. See chapter 7 for more about how charities specifically work with the poor.

USAID well in Cambodia

© Dale Hanson Bourke

Does all the foreign aid really make a difference? Isn't it true that for all the money spent on foreign aid, we could have just handed every poor person a thousand dollars and solved the problem?

■ Some people look at the amount of money spent compared to the number of poor people in the world and think that simply dividing up the money and handing it out might make some sense. But strange as it sounds, cash wouldn't really solve the problems of the poor. Perhaps short term, cash would offer an immediate opportunity to buy food or shelter. But many poor people do not have access to banks, stores, or schools. It isn't enough to alleviate individual poverty if the person lives in a country so poor that systems don't exist to give the person a means to move out of poverty longer term.

Perhaps it is helpful to look at the residents of New Orleans when Hurricane Katrina struck. Their immediate need was relief to escape the high water and to receive food, clean water, and shelter. Some agencies handed out cash to alleviate their immediate problems. But after the initial days, people needed to find places to live, schools for their children, and longer term housing. They needed infrastructure that could only be provided by government or other agencies. Their individual problems could not be solved simply by cash.

Isn't poverty relative? Don't we all feel poor at times relative to others who have more?

■ Poverty is generally measured in relation to a country's average income and the cost of basic goods. If a family's income falls below that level, called the poverty line, a person or family is considered "poor."

The poverty threshold, or poverty line, is the level of income below which one cannot afford to purchase all the resources one requires to live. People who have an income below the poverty line have no discretionary income. The official or common definition of "poverty line" in advanced nations like the United States is much higher than in poorer countries.

In the US, the poverty line for a family of four was $20,000 in 2006, according to the Department of Health and Human Services. That's $5,000 per person per year compared to the $365 per year or less that each of the world's extremely poor live on.

Whether a person feels rich or poor depends on the community in which he or she lives. Even in the poorest villages, some people are still identified as poorer by others, often because they cannot work or

© Raphael Palma, World Vision

AIDS education for women in Bangladesh. Education and empowerment are key to helping women protect themselves against the virus.

provide for themselves or their families. And people who live in wealthy countries may feel poor even though their income is considerably above the median if they live in particularly affluent communities.

What is the Third World?

■ The term was first used in the 1950s during the Cold War to distinguish countries that were not aligned with the West or the Soviet Bloc. Today, however, the term is frequently used to denote nations that are poor, not industrialized, or low on the development index as measured by the UN. There is no objective definition of Third World and in academic and development circles the use of the term is sometimes considered pejorative. It is more acceptable to call such countries "developing countries" or the global South. Sometimes the countries are referred to as the "Two-Thirds World" to make the point that they actually make up the majority of the world.

Is there a First and Second World?

■ Historically, the First World countries were the industrialized countries which embraced capitalism and the Second World countries were those in the communist bloc. More recently, these terms are used to broadly define the richest, most industrialized countries as First World and the emerging economies as Second World. But these definitions are not particularly meaningful when such countries as China and India, though still poor in per capita terms, are poised to become some of the largest economies in the world because of their rapid growth and large populations.

Is India a poor country or a rich country?

■ It is both. India's economy is the second fastest growing in the world, placing it as the twelfth largest economy when measured in GDP. But because of its large population, India's per capita income is just over $3,300.

The recent economic developments have mainly helped upper and middle class Indians. Nearly 35 percent of India's poorest population still lives on less than US$1 a day and almost 80 percent live on less than US$2 per day. India has a high rate of illiteracy and has the highest number of HIV-positive people in the world.

What is a developing country?

■ A developing country is one in which the majority lives on far less money—and often lacks basic public services—than the population in highly-industrialized countries. Five out of the world's six billion people live in developing countries where incomes average less than $2 per day.

Do countries ever move from developing to developed?

■ Yes, many countries have made progress toward becoming developed countries, especially in the post-colonial era. Examples of countries that are now considered developed include Singapore, South Korea, Taiwan, and Greece. A number of countries would be considered well on the way to developed, including Turkey, Brazil, and Thailand. Generally there are some common factors associated with overall progress in development, including: economic growth, good governance, a strong private sector, equitable access to health and education,

> **"Poverty means working more than 18 hours a day, but still not earning enough to feed myself, my husband and my children."**
>
> A poor woman in Cambodia
> (*Voices of the Poor*)

freedom of expression, and the ability to participate in governance.

Are all developed countries democracies?

■ Yes, virtually all developed countries are now democracies. Many developing countries are also now democracies, though their democratic institutions may be fragile and their democratic practices weak.

Freedom House, a research institute headquartered in Washington, D.C., publishes an annual report on democracies in the world, rating them as "free," "somewhat free," or "not free."

What are the largest economies in the world?

■ Measured in Gross Domestic Product, the US is nearly three times the size of the next largest economy, with $11.7 trillion in 2005. Next is Japan with $4.4 trillion, Germany with $2 trillion, Great Britain at $1.7 trillion, followed by France at $1.5 trillion and Italy at $1.2 trillion. China is expected to join

FACT:

More than 100 million primary school-age children are too poor to go to school, according to the World Bank.

A corrugated iron dwelling in South Africa. The inhabitants were unemployed and unable to find work.

the "trillionairs" soon if its economy continues to grow, even though its per capita income is still less than 10 percent of the US, and India is also heading toward a higher GDP.

What are "newly industrialized countries" and "emerging market economies"?

■ Economies that grew fast, especially in East Asia, such as South Korea, Singapore, and Taiwan, used to be called newly industrialized countries or NICs. Countries that are active participants in global financial markets are emerging market economies or EMEs. They include Argentina, Brazil, Thailand, Turkey, and some countries in Central and Eastern Europe. India and China are sometimes included in this grouping, even though they are so much poorer in per capita terms because they are growing so fast and are major players in global markets.

When people talk about human rights violations, what do they mean? Is there a list somewhere of specific human rights?

■ In 1948, the United Nations General Assembly approved the Universal Declaration of Human Rights (UDHR). There have been a number of additional documents since then to further explain and detail various rights. The 28 articles of the current UDHR range from the right to "life, liberty, and security" to the more recent protection of intellectual property rights. It supports equal protection under the law, freedom from slavery, and the right to a "standard of living adequate for the health and well-being of himself and his family. . . ."

" The issue of poverty is not a statistical issue. It is a human issue."

Former World Bank President
James Wolfensohn

Of course, this declaration is controversial to some and considered idealistic by others. Citizens of different countries may or may not experience these rights as a reality and some countries do not protect these rights in their constitution or legal code. There is sometimes disagreement about cultural norms and whether certain practices, such as arranged marriages, should prevail over the human rights declaration that marriage should be entered into freely and with the full consent of both parties.

Do poor people have the same human rights as the rich?

■ One of the basic tenets of the UDHR is that they apply to rich and poor equally. But the reality is that many poor people don't even know their rights or have the means to ask for them.

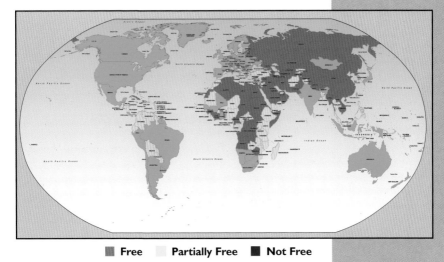

■ Free   Partially Free   ■ Not Free

Freedom House map of democracies in the world.

© Freedom House, Inc.

Who prosecutes those who violate human rights?

■ Gross violations of human rights, such as genocide, are prosecuted by the International Criminal Court (ICC) in The Hague, which was established in 2002.

Why is there so much emphasis on helping women in developing countries?

■ In most poor countries, women and girls have fewer rights, less access to education, and poorer health than men. Mostly because of these factors, especially their lack of rights in relationships, HIV infections are now greater among women than men in Africa. Evidence shows that expanding opportunities for girls and women not only improves their position in society, but it also has a major impact on the overall effectiveness of development. Evidence also shows that when women and men are relatively equal, economies tend to grow faster, the poor move more quickly out of poverty, and the well-being of men, women, and children is enhanced. Studies show that the education of mothers improves the

A poor African child outside his home.

© Clésio DaGama/stock.xchng

health of their children and lowers the fertility rate. Studies also show that when women have more control over the family's income or productive assets, the family's overall situation improves.

Which countries are the poorest in the world?

■ The poorest countries in the world are all found in Africa, which is why there is so much emphasis on assistance to that continent. Using the Human Development Index, the poorest countries in the world in 2006 were: Mozambique, Burundi, Ethiopia, Chad, Central African Republic, Guinea-Bissau, Burkina Faso, Mali, Sierra Leone, and Niger.

What are the Millennium Development Goals and what do they have to do with most Americans?

■ The Millennium Development Goals were adopted in September 2000 by the member states of the United Nations and aim to significantly reduce poverty by 2015. They represent a measurable way to achieve development goals within a timeframe. In other words, instead of simply expressing a goal of reducing global poverty, the goals define the causes of poverty and identify steps that can be taken to eliminate or reduce them by a particular date. Since such organizations as The World Bank, The World Health Organization, and member governments have all signed on to these goals, they represent a commitment by the international community to a unified vision, an agreed upon framework, and a common commitment to particular goals. (See page 107 for a listing of the Millennium Development Goals.)

Slums in São Paulo, Brazil.

THE BIG PICTURE

Even if you never studied economics, it quickly becomes clear that understanding poverty requires a basic knowledge of economic principles and terms. Most people study economics from the perspective of the rich. Here is an overview with an eye toward the poor.

What is capitalism?

■ Capitalism, at its most basic, is the investment of money with the expectation of making a profit. It is money put to work to make more money. Capitalism is generally viewed as an economic system in which the means of production are mostly privately owned and profit flows to an individual or group of individuals. Capitalism is usually considered to involve the right of individuals and groups of individuals acting as "legal persons" (or corporations) to trade in a free market.

Capitalism is sometimes criticized because profit depends on containing labor costs and promoting consumption and it tends to concentrate wealth in the hands of a few. At its worst, a capitalist system exploits labor and promotes materialism. At its best, a capitalist system protects workers while providing opportunities for them to move up the economic ladder. The very poor often lack access to capital, limiting their economic opportunities. Microfinance (see page 103) is one way of providing small sums of money to the working poor so that they can invest it and make a profit.

What is social capital?

■ Social capital is a term used to mean the advantage a person has by living in a society and having informal or formal relationships with people. If a person belongs to a country club, he or she has the advantage of relating to wealthy and powerful people, and therefore receives social capital from simply having access to that environment and membership. Social capital also relates to access or relationships formed in places of worship, educational institutions, and workplaces.

In general, the poor have little social capital. They rarely have opportunities to move up in the world through contacts they make or through social networking. One of the advantages of microfinance, or the system in which small loans are made to the poor, is the social groups formed in what are sometimes called trust banks. Trust banks are groups formed when individuals come together to share their hopes, plans and obstacles, and typically borrow money together, then repay it as a group. By guaranteeing their loans together, they spread out the risk factors associated with individuals and bond as a group, both economically and socially.

What is globalization?

■ Globalization simply describes the growing interrelatedness of countries and cultures, most often economically. Some would say the process began centuries ago when explorers first ventured out to find trading partners. Colonization was another form of globalization that resulted in one country dominating others.

Today, globalization is described by some people as positive and others as negative. Some believe globalization represents hope for the poorest people of the world; others see globalization as modern day imperialism. Globalization tends to homogenize culture, such as when American television shows pervade other countries. But globalization also provides diversity, bringing crafts from developing countries to market in a suburban American shopping mall.

> **"The true capitalist is motivated by the amoral accumulation of money and this frequently drives particular individuals to bend or break the rules."**
>
> James Fulcher in
> *Capitalism*

Technology has increased the rate at which the connections occur. The Internet has created an international bazaar for goods and a global bulletin board of information.

Those who support globalization say it is creating opportunities for people in all parts of the world and improving understanding among different cultures. Those who oppose it say it destroys indigenous cultures and leads to domination by Western economies and cultures.

What is anti-globalization?

■ Anti-globalization describes the political stance of people and groups who oppose certain aspects of globalization, especially the domination of powerful corporations and their influence on global trade agreements and trade-governing bodies (such as the World Trade Organization). There are various groups representing a variety of concerns, including labor rights, environmental protection, developing world issues, and even animal rights.

"Anti-globalization" is considered by many to be a social movement, while others consider it to

FACT:

Twenty percent of the population in the developed world consumes 86 percent of the world's goods.

Various groups take issue with the World Bank and the IMF over their policies relating to poor countries.

be an umbrella term that encompasses a number of separate social movements.

No Logo, a book written by Canadian journalist Naomi Klein and published in 2000, is seen by some as a manifesto of the anti-globalization movement. In the book, Klein criticized such brands as GAP, Nike, and McDonalds, helping make them a target during protests.

What is debt relief?

■ Debt relief is the partial or total forgiveness of debt or the slowing or stopping of debt growth, owed by individuals, corporations, or nations. Debt relief for heavily indebted and underdeveloped countries was first made popular during the 1990s under the banner of Jubilee 2000 and has continued to be a theme of the "Make Poverty History"/ONE campaign. As a result of Jubilee 2000, the Heavily Indebted Poor Countries (HIPC) initiative was launched by the World Bank and the International Monetary Fund to provide systematic debt relief for the poorest countries, while measures were also put into place to ensure the money would be spent on poverty reduction.

The HIPC initiative includes the requirement for countries to have implemented a Poverty Reduction Strategy in agreement with the World Bank and IMF for at least one year.

The Multilateral Debt Relief Initiative (MDRI) is an extension of HIPC. The MDRI came about as a result of the "Make Poverty History"/ONE campaign and was agreed to following the G8's Gleneagles meeting in 2005. It offers 100 percent cancellation of multilateral debts owed by HIPC countries to the World Bank, IMF and African Development Bank.

What is unpayable debt?

■ Unpayable debt is a term used to describe external debt where the principal and interest on the debt are so high given a country's income that it cannot service the debt.

In the many countries, laws prevent banks from making loans to individuals who do not "qualify," meaning their income is not sufficient to service the debt on their loan without endangering their ability to provide for basic needs.

What is odious debt?

■ Odious debt is defined as a debt that is incurred by a regime for purposes not in the interest of the state. For example, if a ruler borrows money in the name of his country, but then uses the funds to build a personal palace or build his military rather than helping pay for the public needs of his country, it is considered odious debt. Such debts are considered to be personal debts of the regime, not debts of the state.

Sadly, the debt of many developing countries is tied to corrupt leadership and odious debt which benefited the ruler but not the people.

What is fair trade?

■ Fair trade is a movement which promotes equitable standards for labor and helps preserve the environment, especially on products exported from developing countries to the developed world. Although there is more than one organization labeling products as "fair trade" certified, the largest groups have joined together in an organization to promote the same interests.

© TransFairUSA

The symbol of TransFair USA, one of the organizations that certifies products.

Fair trade's goal is to work with poor workers and help them develop economic self-sufficiency as well as to help reform international trade standards and make them more sensitive to issues in developing markets. In general that means making sure workers and producers get a fair wage or fair payment for crops, that their working conditions are safe and healthy, that women's work is valued and children are not exploited, and that the environment is not harmed.

What are property rights?

■ Very simply, property rights are the legal protection to own and protect physical or intellectual assets. Typically that includes the right to control, benefit from, sell, or exclude others from your property.

Peruvian economist Hernando De Soto contends that one of the main reasons the poor are trapped in poverty is because they do not legally own the property they often hold. Most of the poor either farm land that isn't theirs or are squatters in shanty towns without title to their land. In his book, *The Mystery of Capital*, De Soto claims the value of real estate held but not legally owned by the poor is at least $9.3 trillion.

While critics claim he is overstating the amount, his point is clear: Without formal title to their property, poor people lack security and the ability to leverage their property to borrow or move up in the economy. They have limited incentives to invest in their property and little ability to plan for their future. Without the ability to pass property to their children, the cycle of poverty continues from generation to generation.

De Soto also points out that the primary way wealth has been built in a country like the US is through property ownership and the ability to pass property on to heirs.

What are economic sanctions and why are they imposed?

■ Economic sanctions are penalties imposed on a country by another country or group of countries because of economic or political decisions that are considered injurious. Sanctions may include tariffs, restrictions on trade, duties, or quotas. Economic sanctions between countries can result in trade wars and are arbitrated by the WTO as the governing body for trade disputes between countries.

The UN imposed economic sanctions on Iraq in order to force the government to comply with UN weapons inspections. The US imposed sanctions on India after it proceeded with nuclear tests. But the US has also imposed economic sanctions on countries that are seen as "dumping" goods in the US in a way that harms US producers. These sanctions may, and often are, protested to the WTO.

What is meant by protectionism?

■ Protectionism refers to a country imposing tariffs or other fees on goods from other countries in an effort to protect businesses or workers within its borders from the competition of cheaper or higher quality foreign goods and services. The US is not generally a protectionist country, except with respect to its agriculture. American consumers can buy a wide variety of foreign imports.

What happened to NAFTA?

■ The North American Free Trade Agreement was signed into law in 1992 among much fanfare and controversy. It basically removed restrictions in trade among the US, Canada, and Mexico and created a free trade zone in North America.

Labor unions opposed it, believing cheaper labor in Mexico would mean a loss of jobs. But Mexico has also claimed that US subsidies for agriculture have really negated the benefits to Mexican agriculture and created an unfair advantage. There is also a belief that NAFTA hurts trade between the US and the rest of the world.

NAFTA continues to be in effect and continues to draw both criticism and praise.

What is green economics?

■ Green economics believes that any measure of economic interest should begin with the ecosystem and the impact on it. While most economists see the ecosystem as external to economic activity, green economics changes the entire way activity is measured.

Green economics views the ecosystem as limited, therefore is concerned about limiting growth. It also views all activities as interconnected and emphasizes impacts on the environment.

© Dale Hanson Bourke

Pollution from copper mines in northern Zambia.

Green parties are very popular in many countries, and increasingly so in the developing world.

How do environmental issues impact the poor?

■ There is a growing understanding that the poor are severely impacted by pollution, global warming, and environmental degradation. Without the power to legally protect their environment, the poor often live in the dumping grounds, where the rich have relegated their garbage or located their polluting businesses. In addition, the poor often have to live off the land and access water from public waterways, resources increasingly contaminated by fertilizer, industrial run off, and public disposal.

Natural disasters are often exacerbated by overcrowding, poor soil conditions, deforestation, and other conditions common to regions where the poor live.

What are tariffs? Do they hurt poor countries?

■ A tariff is simply a tax on imported goods. A tariff is often applied to foreign goods to help protect the market for nationally-produced products. Some economists believe that the US, European countries, Canada, and Australia use tariffs unfairly against developing countries where some goods, especially agricultural, can be made for less.

The WTO is a group of nations that generally opposes tariffs and supports free trade principles that allow countries to trade with one another without discriminating against countries that can produce goods at lower prices.

FACT:

Most African countries only gained independence in the last 50 years.

What are subsidies?

■ A subsidy is a form of government assistance to an industry to encourage the production of a commodity. It may take the form of a tax break, grant or the creation of a trade barrier, to protect the producer from foreign competition.

A tariff may be imposed on foreign goods as a type of subsidy to a national industry.

Is outsourcing really hurting our economy? Is it helping others?

■ Outsourcing simply means that a company contracts or transfers part of its business to another entity. Generally, the word is associated with corporations sending their business overseas, where they can access less expensive and more available labor pools. Technically, that would be called offshore outsourcing.

While most economists don't believe the practice hurts the economy as a whole, it does substitute jobs in the US for jobs overseas and hurts pockets of labor. But because it reduces costs to corporations, it ultimately helps business grow which fuels the economy.

Offshore outsourcing does provide much needed jobs to workers in other countries. Both India and China have profited from the influx of work from other countries.

What is meant by public health?

■ The focus of public health is to prevent disease in a population. In a country like the US, this means that the Surgeon General works with the Centers for Disease Control and Prevention (CDC) to recommend and institute country wide vaccination, testing and other programs to prevent epidemics and promote wellness. The US government spends approximately $5,000 per person on this objective.

In poor countries there is little access to health care and public health functions are either minimal or nonexistent. As a result, diseases which could be easily prevented are never addressed and can become country wide epidemics, and even simple information, such as how to treat a baby who has diarrhea, is never disseminated.

Many poor countries have poor health systems and few doctors and medical staff. To fill this gap, international non-governmental organizations often step in.

FACT:

Just one week of subsidies given to farmers in the developed world would cover the annual cost of food aid.

Selling fruit and vegetables at a local Dominican market helps this man provide for his family, but does not return much profit.

Rainy season often destroys fragile homes, cuts people off from roads, and offers breeding grounds for malarial mosquitoes.

NATURE VERSUS MAN

Nature is not always kind to the poor. They lack information to anticipate disasters, transportation to flee, and the reserves to start over again. What would be natural cycles to those in the developed world are a series of disasters to the poor. Understanding these basic forces helps explain the underlying causes of chronic poverty.

Why are so many people starving? Isn't there enough food in the world?

■ Actually, there is plenty of food in the world to feed every person, yet more than 800 million people are chronically hungry. Hunger and poverty are responsible for approximately 25,000 deaths each day according to the UN World Food Program.

The problem is not food production, but food availability. In many parts of the world, people do not have access to adequate quantities of food or food with sound nutritional value. Many poor people fill their stomachs with starches, such as maize or rice, that provide few nutrients. Poor people cannot adequately protect themselves against nature's cycles, so have a hard time preserving food for times of drought. They have limited ability to irrigate dry soil or protect crops against the hot sun or invading pests. Wars further disrupt people's ability to grow crops or find ongoing food supplies. And environmental factors, such as soil erosion and water pollution, are also harmful to food production. In some parts of the world, the deserts are encroaching more and more on once productive land.

Why can't rich countries just ship food to the poor?

■ The wealthy countries of the world provide regular food aid to the poorer countries. This is especially true in times of famine or other disasters. But it is extremely difficult for food to reach people in the most outlying areas where there are few roads or nearby airports. And food aid is not a sustainable solution.

One of the problems with providing assistance in times of disaster is that local food production can be hurt or delayed because of the availability of donated food. Local farmers and food producers lose their market when free food is available, delaying their ability to recover from famines or other disasters. One way around this is to offer vouchers for people to buy food from local suppliers.

USAID Famine Alert Levels

■ **EMERGENCY**

A significant food security crisis is occurring, where portions of the population are now, or will soon become, extremely food insecure and face imminent famine. Decision makers should give the highest priority to responding to the situations highlighted by this Emergency alert.

■ **WARNING**

A food crisis is developing, where groups are now, or about to become, highly food insecure and take increasingly irreversible actions that undermine their future food security. Decision makers should urgently address the situations highlighted by this Warning.

■ **WATCH**

There are indications of a possible food security crisis. Decision makers should pay increasing attention to the situations highlighted in this Watch, and update preparedness and contingency planning measures to address the situation.

■ **NO ALERT**

There are no indications of Food Security problems.

What is famine?

- A famine occurs when a large percentage of the population of a region or country is so undernourished that death by starvation is common. Famine occurs primarily in developing countries and mostly in Africa. It is usually caused by crop failures, insect infestations, or drought, especially in regions without reserves or the ability to purchase additional food from other areas. It is often associated with wars or disease, especially when people are not able to regularly tend their land and crops.

Although there is no technical measure to determine whether crop failure is massive enough to be called a famine, USAID posts a famine alert system on its website, ranging from "watch" to "emergency."

What is malnutrition?

- Malnutrition occurs when there is an extended period of little food or food of little nutritious value. It usually refers to inadequate consumption, poor absorption, or excessive loss of nutrients. A person experiences malnutrition if the appropriate amount of food or quality of nutrients are not consumed for an extended period of time. Eventually, malnutrition may result in starvation.

Malnourished people either do not have enough calories, or are eating a diet that lacks protein, vitamins, or trace minerals. Medical problems arising from

© Dale Hanson Bourke

FACT:

Six million children under five die every year of malnutrition.

This young Cambodian boy shows signs of malnutrition.

malnutrition are called deficiency diseases. Poor people often rely heavily on starchy foods which help them feel less hungry, but do not necessarily provide adequate nutrition. Eye diseases, scurvy ,and other problems often occur in poor countries because people lack vitamins. UNICEF estimates that a million children a year die from lack of Vitamin A. Lack of iron may be responsible for the death of 300 women a day who die in childbirth according to the WHO.

What is food security?

■ Food security simply means people are not chronically hungry or near starvation. According to the UN, approximately 852 million men, women, and children are chronically hungry due to extreme poverty, and as many as 2 billion people lack food because they are poor.

Families with financial resources rarely suffer from chronic hunger. Poor families not only suffer the most from chronic hunger but are also most at risk during food shortages and famines.

The UN's Food and Agriculture Organization (FAO) defines food security as: "when all people, at all times, have access to sufficient, safe, and nutritious food to meet their dietary needs and food preferences for an active and healthy life."

According to the US Department of Agriculture, "food security for a household means access by all members at all times to enough food for an active, healthy life. Food security includes at a minimum (1) the ready availability of nutritionally adequate and safe foods, and (2) an assured ability to acquire acceptable foods in socially acceptable ways (that is, without resorting to emergency food supplies, scavenging, stealing, or other coping strategies)."

It seems like famines continue to occur in the same countries. Why can't the countries anticipate and deal with these problems? Or why don't people move to better places?

- It's true that some regions of the world are more prone to droughts and crop failures due to their geography. Without massive irrigation, many parts of the US and other developed countries would also suffer droughts. Because of the ability to bring water to dry areas, guard against insects, and protect from other pests, crops grow successfully in many regions.

But poor countries often lack the ability to develop irrigation systems or even to access fresh water sources. And crops are most often grown to support a family or a village instead of as cash crops (crops sold to others for income), leaving few resources to invest in long term improvement or planning.

Once crops are harvested it is difficult for poor people to store food safely. There is rarely any refrigeration or even a dry place free of insects. So it is difficult to store up food for leaner times, meaning people are dependent on the immediate crop and tend to live from harvest to harvest.

Millions of poor people move annually in the hope of finding a better life—from rural to urban areas or from poor to rich countries. But some of

Survivors of the eruption from Mount Nyiragongo in the Democratic Republic of the Congo

FACT:

Approximately 853 million men, women and children are chronically hungry due to extreme poverty.

the extreme poor are literally too poor to buy the bus ticket or fear ethnic discrimination in other regions or cannot expect to find a job because they speak another language.

People who move are also sometimes forced out by war or other disasters. And even in developed countries, those who leave a difficult situation first are those who have the means to do so.

Wouldn't things be better if people had fewer children?

■ It's true that poor women often have more children than women living in developed countries, but the reasons for this are complex. Children are dependents but are also the greatest assets a poor family has. At an early age, they begin to help with family chores and soon help work to feed their families by fishing, helping raise crops or animals, or working in the family business.

Children provide security for families by caring for their parents when they grow old and helping care for brothers and sisters or nieces or nephews who are sick or in need. Family members are the only safety net most poor people have.

In addition, in many poor countries, a woman knows that she may lose a number of her children at birth or during early childhood. Infant mortality rates in poor countries are very high; the number of children who die before their fifth birthday is even higher. Family planning, including birth control, is not available or practiced in some poor countries.

Economic development is often called the most effective family planning tool because as people feel more secure and women have more opportunity for education, birth rates almost always decline. Still, making health and family planning services available does tend to lead to lower birth rates.

Why do so many babies die?

■ Infant mortality statistics are sometimes difficult to verify since many women do not officially register births at all or wait until the child reaches one year of age. But infant mortality rates for most countries measure the number of children who are born in a year divided by the number of deaths of children under the age of one. Most babies die in the first year because of dehydration, diarrhea, and disease.

Statistics for infant mortality are measured per 1000 births so they can be compared by country. In some poor countries, an average of one out of five babies does not survive the first year. In addition, more than half a million poor women die in childbirth each year.

Why do so many children under the age of five die?

■ According to UNICEF, more than 10 million children die every year from preventable causes. That's more than 30,000 children each day. Causes include disease—especially pneumonia, malaria, and HIV/AIDS—as well as malnutrition, lack of

burp

TIME TO MAKE AN APPOINTMENT FOR LIPOSUCTION.

REPORT: THE NUMBER OF OVERWEIGHT PEOPLE IN THE WORLD EQUALS THE NUMBER OF MALNOURISHED PEOPLE.

In malarial regions of Africa, only 1 out of every 20 people own a bed net.

access to clean water, diarrhea, and lack of sanitation.

In countries like Sierra Leone, three children out of ten die before their fifth birthday.

Because the poor lack medicine or access to health care, even a curable disease can cause fever, dehydration, and death. And lack of a bed net to keep malaria-infected mosquitoes off a sleeping child and safe spraying to reduce mosquito populations means millions of children are infected with this potentially deadly disease each year. Despite international efforts, too few have access to drugs to cure it.

Does the US have the highest rate of child survival?

■ The US has one of the better rates in the world, but actually ranks behind a number of countries, including Canada, the UK, Japan, Germany, Australia, and even Korea and Singapore.

What is life expectancy and how is it measured?

■ Technically, life expectancy means the expected number of years remaining to live at a given age. It is often compared across countries at time of birth. Because of factors like high infant mortality, a child at birth has a certain life expectancy, which rises as he or she passes the age of five. In the aggregate, life expectancy is one measure of a country's standard of living.

Life expectancy at birth varies from Japan, where it is 81, to Swaziland, where it has fallen to 33, primarily due to HIV/AIDS.

Although life expectancy was increasing for many years (and continues to increase in many countries), countries affected by HIV/AIDS have shown an alarming trend toward a decreasing life expectancy.

Ironically, some experts see life expectancy in some developing countries beginning to slow because of obesity and related conditions which are becoming a significant public health threat.

Should we still be concerned about over population in the world?

■ Some people advocate population control, primarily by reducing the birth rate. While those who advocate the policy have generally encouraged it as a voluntary practice, governments, such as China and India have had, in the past, restrictive policies that are considered a violation of human rights. Some proponents point to studies showing high birth rates among the poor tend to correlate to poor economic conditions. Others claim it is impossible to correlate the two factors.

Groups opposing birth control, such as the Catholic Church, have fought against the notion of the world being in danger of over population. Others have seen it as a movement by rich countries to restrict the number of poor people in the world and claim it is a form of imperialism. Critics have argued that overpopulation is not a problem in developed countries and with pandemics like malaria and HIV/AIDS claiming millions of lives in the developing world, overpopulation is not a problem in poor countries either.

Groups that were once very vocal about over population issues have changed their focus to advocate for women's rights in birth control, marriage, and literacy; all issues affecting the birth rates in many countries. Studies do show that as countries become more developed and women have more rights, birth rates tend to slow.

FACT:

World population now exceeds 6.45 billion people.

Why is it so hard for people to get clean water?

■ Only 2.5 percent of water on the Earth is fresh water, and more than two thirds of that is frozen. Water demand exceeds supply in much of the world, including developed countries. California, for example, receives most of its water supply from other states.

But many people do not have the ability to bring water from one place to another efficiently or to store water for droughts. In some villages, women spend much of their day walking to a source of water, filling their buckets, and bringing the water back to the village. To some people, the "rainy season," when rains fill ponds and streams, provides the only water for the rest of the year. For months after the rains end, women dip their buckets into fetid water and livestock drink and walk in the same water.

Some aid organizations concentrate on drilling wells to help provide access to clean water. But depending on the geography of the region, wells may need to be dug through hard rock or may require more than a hand pump to draw the water out of the well.

Other sources of clean water are becoming polluted by industry, run off from fields, or use by livestock and humans of the same bodies of water for bathing and drinking water.

What does AIDS have to do with poverty?

■ Poverty relates to HIV/AIDS in many ways. Those who are poor are often malnourished and in poor health. They easily contract malaria and tuberculosis, making them even more susceptible to HIV infections. Women are often infected in poor countries because they have little power to resist sexual advances or to insist on protection if their husband is infected. Some women are so poor that they trade sex for food, especially if their children are starving.

Men are also victims of poverty, often having to travel to another country to work for months at a time and often going to local prostitutes. Men who worked as truckers in Africa helped spread the HIV infections as they moved from major city to major city, frequenting prostitutes and spreading the disease across Africa.

Is AIDS really such a big problem?

■ Each year, AIDS kills nearly 3 million people, mostly in poor countries. Worldwide, nearly 40 million people are infected, with the vast majority living in sub-Saharan Africa. In Africa alone, there are 12 million AIDS orphans.

Many scientists believe that HIV, the virus that causes AIDS, first appeared in Africa and continued, unabated, for years before it was identified. Because so many people die in Africa from malaria, tuberculosis, and other disease, AIDS was not noticed as a unique cause of death. In fact, many people who

Adults and children estimated to be living with HIV in 2005.

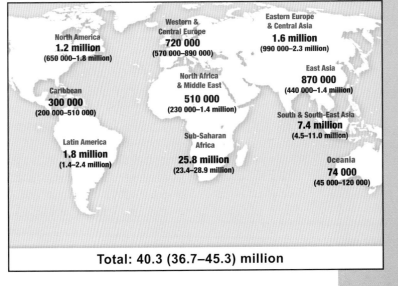

North America
1.2 million
(650 000–1.8 million)

Western & Central Europe
720 000
(570 000–890 000)

Eastern Europe & Central Asia
1.6 million
(990 000–2.3 million)

North Africa & Middle East
510 000
(230 000–1.4 million)

East Asia
870 000
(440 000–1.4 million)

Caribbean
300 000
(200 000–510 000)

Latin America
1.8 million
(1.4–2.4 million)

Sub-Saharan Africa
25.8 million
(23.4–28.9 million)

South & South-East Asia
7.4 million
(4.5–11.0 million)

Oceania
74 000
(45 000–120 000)

Total: 40.3 (36.7–45.3) million

© UNAIDS/WHO

are HIV infected die of other diseases because their immune systems are compromised.

A person may be infected by HIV for as many as ten years without showing symptoms, although he or she is still infectious. This means that people who do not have access to testing may be infecting others for years before they develop full blown AIDS. Women often first discover they are infected after giving birth to a child who has HIV/AIDS.

Women are often forced to marry at a young age when their bodies are immature and more prone to infection. They typically are married to an older man who has already had sex partners or visited prostitutes and is highly likely to be infected.

A woman who has a sexually transmitted disease or other vaginal infections is also more likely to be infected with HIV. And if she is undernourished, her body has less ability to fight the infection or resist other diseases. If a person is infected with malaria, he or she is also less resistant to HIV infection.

Why do so many people get malaria in poor countries but not in wealthy countries?

■ Malaria once was a problem in Europe and the US. In fact, the District of Columbia, which was quite swampy in the 1800s, had a high rate of malaria infections. Before the Panama Canal could be built, a program to eradicate malaria and yellow fever was undertaken so successfully that the tropical zone became free of disease within a year. Malaria was eliminated from the northern parts of the US in the early twentieth century, and the use of the pesticides, including DDT, eliminated it from the South by 1951. In the 1950s and 1960s, there was a major public health effort to eradicate malaria worldwide, which worked in some countries but not in most of the developing world.

Malaria is endemic in a broad band around the equator, which happens to coincide with many of the poorest countries in the world. But it is worst in sub-Saharan Africa, where nearly 90 percent of fatalities from the disease occur. In some regions, malaria is only present during the rainy season and is more common in rural areas than cities.

Malaria causes about 350–500 million infections in humans and approximately one to three million deaths annually, but because most infections occur in areas where people have little access to health care, the numbers are difficult to verify. The vast majority of cases occur in children under the age of 5 years. Every 30 seconds an African child dies of malaria. Pregnant women are also especially vulnerable.

Malaria is not just a disease commonly associated with poverty, it is also a major hindrance to economic development. The economic impact of malaria has been estimated to cost Africa $12 billion each year.

© Dale Hanson Bourke

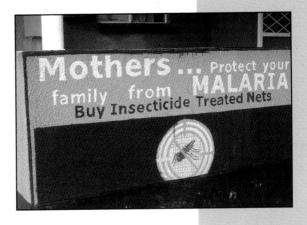

This sign, painted on the wall of a clinic in Africa, helps raise awareness of the number one killer of children on the continent.

Why are is there so much attention being given to malaria now?

■ In 2006, President Bush launched the President's Malaria Initiative (PMI) in order to lead a campaign to wipe out malaria. Because of that effort and the involvement of groups like Malaria No More, much more attention is being given to this preventable disease.

Simple interventions like mosquito nets help keep mosquitoes away from people, especially when treated with an insecticide. Insecticide-treated nets (ITNs) are estimated to be twice as effective as untreated nets. The nets cost around 5 dollars each. Unfortunately, most poor people can't afford to pay even that amount, and only one out of 20 people in Africa owns a bed net. So much of the effort is going to help supply nets to people.

Another intervention, now approved by the WHO, is targeted use of DDT. DDT was developed as the first of the modern insecticides and initially used to combat malaria. But awareness of the consequences of large-scale use led to its ban in many countries, and by then, some mosquitoes had developed a tolerance to it.

Some advocates claim that bans are responsible for tens of millions of deaths in tropical countries where previously DDT was effective in controlling malaria.

Why is tuberculosis such a problem in the developing world?

■ Tuberculosis, commonly called "TB" killed nearly 2 million people in 2005, almost all in developing countries. Worldwide, approximately 15 million people have active TB, but millions more carry the disease in their systems and will eventually develop an active case of the disease.

TB infections are on the rise worldwide, especially in developing countries. TB and HIV/AIDS are often called the "terrible twins" because when a person's immune system is depressed by HIV or AIDS, tuberculosis often emerges from the latent form or a person is easily infected by airborne bacteria.

In 1993 the WHO declared TB a global health emergency because of the rising rate of infections and deaths and the emergence of drug-resistant strains of the disease. A particularly lethal and so far drug-resistant form of tuberculosis, called XDTB, is now found in parts of southern Africa.

> "Poverty doesn't produce unhappiness—it produces degradation."
>
> George Bernard Shaw

Can poor people get insurance to help them recover from floods or other disasters?

- Insurance is an important factor to those living in developed countries. It protects individuals from forces of nature or health crises. Generally, the poor do not have insurance. That is why even a small crisis can become catastrophic and why the cycles of nature are too often devastating to those living on the edge already.

Some organizations are experimenting with providing insurance to the poor, especially in relation to microfinance loans. If the poor are insured against catastrophic loss, they are more likely to invest in the future. If they know their children will be cared for in case of their death or illness, they are more likely to create sustainable businesses. If crops are insured against failure, there is more crop rotation and the land will remain fertile.

Insurance products are one of the most exciting new tools for helping the poor by protecting them from natural disasters and unexpected catastrophes so they can move their families forward.

© Jon Warren, World Vision

Community members participate in search and rescue efforts during devastating flooding in Haiti and the Dominican Republic.

War torn building in Lebanon.

UNNATURAL CAUSES

It is not just floods and famines that assail the poor. Because they are powerless, poor people have few advocates and little access to the law and justice. Being poor means being subjected to various type of violence and disruption. The Millennium Development Goals address the major causes of poverty, both natural and man-made. Here are just some of the factors that create havoc for the poor of the world.

Why are there so many wars and conflicts in poor countries?

■ Poor countries often lack strong leadership, healthy democracies, and adequate infrastructures—including courts—to handle the types of conflicts that occur in daily life. In addition, people in many poor countries must struggle to gain access to water and other natural resources needed for daily life, so it is common for property disputes to occur when such resources are controlled by a few.

In Africa especially, the history of colonialism included pitting ethnic groups against one another in order to gain and maintain control. Several books have documented this, including *King Leopold's Ghost* by Adam Hochschild and *Africa: A Biography of the Continent* by John Reader. When country borders were drawn, tribes and people groups were often purposely divided up to minimize numbers and power.

Natural resources such as oil are another factor creating tension in countries where rights are not clearly established by law and outside forces often fuel control over the resources giving little to the poor people in the country. People are frequently driven out of their homes by wars or natural disasters and make their way into other regions or lands

FACT:

In 2005 there were 39 wars and armed conflicts in the world.

where they are considered outsiders. Sometimes this creates tension in the new land.

What are "fragile states"?

■ Fragile states are countries susceptible to crisis, usually politically, economically, or socially. They have fragile infrastructures and governance models making them vulnerable to both internal and external conflicts. They may become "failed states" if they slide further into chaos. A stable state is one in which the government and internal structures mean a country can withstand problems without threatening the entire framework of the country.

The Fund for Peace publishes an annual index called "The Failed State Index" where it ranks nations based on factors such as demographic pressures; movement of refugees and internally displaced peoples; uneven economic development along group lines; economic decline; deterioration of public services; widespread violation of human rights; and other factors.

The US government has recently pledged more aid and funding to countries considered fragile states to try to help alleviate the need to respond to humanitarian and other disasters that occur in failed states.

What are "blood diamonds"?

■ Blood diamonds, or conflict diamonds, are diamonds mined in a war zone and sold illegally. Blood diamonds first came to the world's attention in the late 1990s, during the violent civil war in Sierra Leone. Rebels attempted to overthrow the government, and an illicit diamond trade was used to fund the war effort. Other countries accused of mining or trafficking in conflict diamonds at various times include Angola, Liberia, Democratic Republic of the Congo, and Ivory Coast.

> " Africa is the most stable of the Earth's continental land masses ... and yet it is also the most divided continent on Earth."
>
> John Reader in
> *Africa, A Biography of a Continent*

In 2000, the diamond producing countries of Africa met in Kimberley, South Africa, to create a way to certify diamonds entering the world market in order to assure buyers that they were not buying conflict diamonds. In 2003, the United States enacted the Clean Diamond Trade Act (CDTA) which made the import of rough diamonds from war zones illegal and created a mechanism to implement what is now called the Kimberley process. Because of that, diamonds bought in the US have to be registered and certified.

Isn't corruption the big problem in many poor countries?

■ Corruption has been a problem and continues to be, but progress is being made. The World Bank considers corruption an obstacle to economic and social development and has instituted a number of policies to ensure the proper use of funds. The US has also created new structures (such as the Millennium Challenge Corporation) which reward countries making progress against corruption and to evaluate and ban funding to countries where corruption

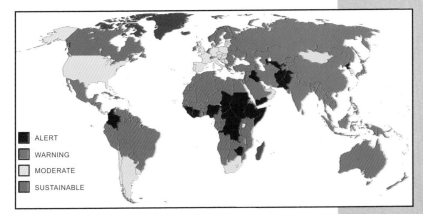

ALERT
WARNING
MODERATE
SUSTAINABLE

© The Fund For Peace

Failed State Index

continues. Debt relief is being made available to a number of countries but the leadership must first prove that the funding will actually go to help the people. Without these assurances and a measurable plan, debt relief is not forthcoming.

What does it mean to be a refugee?

■ A refugee is a person who has left his or her own country and is seeking either temporary shelter or long term asylum in a foreign country. Refugees are typically fleeing war or natural disasters. According to the UN High Commission on Refugees (UNHCR), there are about 9.2 million refugees in the world. Millions of other people have fled their homes but have not crossed national borders. These people are called Internally Displaced Persons or IDPs. They often face similar challenges to refugees, including not only lack of resources, but lack of proper documentation in order to work, attend school, or own property.

What is the difference between a refugee and an immigrant?

■ An immigrant is someone who has left his or her country willingly in order to seek a better life in another nation. An immigrant typically comes to another country intending to make it a permanent home. A refugee may seek asylum or protection for a short or longer period of time. Depending on the country, one or both groups of people may be eligible to become citizens of the new country. Both groups often struggle economically because they may lack communications skills, education, or necessary documents in order to fully participate in society.

How does immigration affect the world economy?

- Historically, immigrants have become some of the best workers and most successful entrepreneurs in their new homes. But the flow of immigrants has been restricted in many of the wealthier nations, creating a smaller number of legal immigrants and a larger number of illegal or undocumented workers.

When you look at the world as a whole, you see that people in wealthier countries are having fewer children and are living longer, creating a labor shortage in industrialized nations. In poorer countries, populations are still growing fast, even though fertility is falling, because of the bulge of young people now having children who were born when fertility rates were higher and infant mortality rates were falling. Without immigrants, many industrialized countries would experience acute labor shortages, especially in such areas as agriculture, service industries, and support jobs in health care.

FACT:

There are 9.2 million refugees in the world.

Origin of Major Refugee Populations as of January 2006 (Ten Largest Groups)

ORIGIN	MAIN COUNTRIES OF ASYLUM	TOTAL[1]
Afghanistan	Pakistan / Iran / Germany / Netherlands / UK	1,908,100[2]
Sudan	Chad / Uganda / Kenya / Ethiopia / Central African Rep.	693,300
Burundi	Tanzania / DR Congo / Rwanda / South Africa / Zambia	438,700
DR Congo	Tanzania / Zambia / Congo / Rwanda / Uganda	430,600
Somalia	Kenya / Yemen / UK / USA / Ethiopia	394,800
Viet Nam	China / Germany / USA / France / Switzerland	358,200
Palestinians	Saudi Arabia / Egypt / Iraq / Libya / Algeria	349,700[3]
Iraq	Iran / Germany / Netherlands / Syria / UK	262,100
Azerbaijan	Armenia / Germany / USA / Netherlands / France	233,700
Liberia	Sierra Leone / Guinea / Côte d'Ivoire / Ghana / USA	231,100

1 This table includes UNHCR estimates for nationalities in industrialized countries on the basis of recent refugee arrivals and asylum-seeker recognition.

2 UNHCR figures for Pakistan only include Afghans living in camps who are assisted by UNHCR. A 2005 government census of Afghans in Pakistan, and subsequent repatriation movements, suggest an additional 1.5 million Afghans—some of whom may be refugees—are living outside camps. The figure for Iran has been revised upwards since 1 January.

3 This figure does not include some 4.3 million Palestinian refugees who come under the separate mandate of the UN Relief and Works Agency for Palestine Refugees in the Near East (UNRWA).

The International Organization for Migration (IOM) estimates that there are as many as 40 million illegal immigrants in industrialized countries. The issue is becoming increasingly acute, since industrialized countries depend on these workers but in many cases do not offer them access to legal status or social services.

What is labor migration?

■ When people cannot find work close to home, they often have to go to other regions or countries in order to find employment to support their families. In Mozambique, for example, many men spend months away from home working in the mines of South Africa. The effects of this are often detrimental to the family and, in the case of Africa, have contributed to the spread of HIV infections because the men often frequent prostitutes.

A very typical example is when a family lives in a village and either or both parents must spend much of their time working in a city. There is often no place for the family to live, so they must be separated for long periods of time.

An example in the US is many domestic workers and nannies who leave their own children in order to care for other people's children and then send their earnings home.

Is it true that the money sent home by foreign workers can contribute substantially to an economy?

■ Money transferred by foreign worker to their home countries are called remittances. According to the World Bank, workers from developing countries sent home more than $160 billion to their families in 2004, contributing substantially to the economies of many countries. In Latin America and the Caribbean, remittances are greater than the combined sum of foreign direct investment and official development.

The top countries in remittances from workers in the US are Mexico ($13.3 billion), India ($5 billion), and the Philippines ($5 billion). Most of that is sent through Western Union and Moneygram.

Why don't the poor own property?

■ There are a variety of reasons people do not have access to property ownership. Often the laws of a country make land ownership difficult for individuals and create confusing systems that can only be negotiated by the educated or wealthy. Families may be living on land they believe is theirs, but may have failed to file documents and the land may be sold without their knowledge. In some countries people may not even be officially citizens because their birth was never registered and therefore they are not eligible to own land.

When you realize the amount of knowledge and assistance it takes to buy property in a country like the US, you begin to understand how someone without education, or access to lawyers can feel powerless about property ownership.

© Dale Hanson Bourke

More than 30,000 children die each day from preventable causes.

A young girl in Uganda works with her family.

How can someone who lives in a country not be a citizen?

■ When people have to leave their country and flee disasters, they often lose any documents establishing their identity. When they arrive in a new country, they may live there illegally or without official status. Their children also may lack official identity because the parents lacked citizenship. Some people are displaced for generations, creating a massive number of non-citizen residents in a country: people who have no vote, no right to property, and no ability to register their children in schools.

Some people live in areas so remote that they have never registered births, deaths, or property. Depending on the laws of the country, they may not be entitled to government services because they are not officially on the government roles.

Is there a link between terrorism and poverty?

■ Some people have hypothesized that chronic poverty and injustice have forced people to resort to terrorism. While it is true that groups of people who are repressed and forced to live in poor conditions may rebel, the best known terrorists have not been poor. Those responsible for the September 11, 2001, attack on the US were mostly middle class. So were the suicide bombers who attacked London in the summer of 2005. On the other hand, fragile and failed states provide safe haven for terrorists groups, such as in Afghanistan.

Some studies have tried to track the correlation between poverty and terrorism but have not been able to establish a verifiable link. Many other factors seem to be involved, and often those who engage in terrorism are not the very poor, but those who have the means to engage in such activities as bomb-making. The poorest of the poor are often so busy simply

> *"For many poor countries, the share of skilled nationals residing in rich countries is staggeringly high."*
>
> Devesh Kapur and John McHale in *Give Us Your Best and Brightest*

surviving that they have little time and energy to launch plans, even if they feel they are being treated unjustly. There is also concern that linking terrorism and poverty implies that the poor are by nature violent or immoral.

But in long term refugee camps, where people have no means of income or escape, anti-social ideas can flourish and unoccupied young people can be tempted to join extremist organizations. Nobel Peace Prize winner Mohammed Yunnis asserts that helping end poverty will help stop terrorism.

What is the black market? Is it always criminal?

■ By definition, the black market or underground market is an illegal economic activity. It may be that the goods themselves are illegal, such as drugs or weapons, or that they are legal goods sold in a way that avoids taxes, licensing, or other fees.

It is estimated that the market for illegal drugs is as much as $400 billion per year. In countries like Afghanistan, Peru, Bolivia, and other poor countries where farmers are encouraged to grow coca for cocaine or poppies for heroin, the difference between growing an illegal cash crop or a legal crop is often the difference between remaining poor or having enough income to provide for their families.

Prostitution is also an illegal activity in many countries (although it is legal in a number of countries in the world). Other black market goods are commodities such as ivory and other animal parts.

What are "sweatshops"?

■ Sweatshops are factories or other workplaces where employees work under poor conditions, work long hours for low pay, suffer unsafe conditions, or are not free to leave or quit at will. The US government defines a sweatshop as any "employer

The market for illegal drugs is as much as $400 billion per year.

that violates more than one federal or state labor law governing minimum wage and overtime, child labor, industrial homework, occupational safety and health, workers' compensation, or industry registration."

Some critics of globalization or offshore outsourcing claim the developing world is being victimized by rich countries seeking to have products made inexpensively overseas. They point out that costs are low because labor is underpaid and overworked in developing countries and the demand creates the environment for sweatshops. But the labor laws in some countries are not the same as in the developed world. Unions rarely exist to seek worker rights. What is viewed as a sweatshop in one country is an opportunity for employment in another. The legal definition of fair working conditions differs from country to country, although there are generally accepted labor standards internationally.

Is it wrong to employ children in most of the world? Isn't it better to give them work than let them remain so poor?

■ The definition of child labor is very broad, ranging from forced and bonded labor or slavery to household chores or work on a family farm. The International Labour Organization (ILO) estimates that 246 million children between the ages of 5 and 17 are engaged in some type of child labor, the majority of which is in unsafe conditions, such as mines or agriculture. UNICEF estimates that more than 8 million children between 5 and 17 are engaged in child labor of the worst kinds: prostitution, slavery, debt bondage, armed conflict, or other illicit activities.

In some countries, it is considered inappropriate or exploitative if a child below a certain age works, except doing household chores. An outside employer is not allowed to hire a child below a certain age in some countries. In the US, the minimum age to work in an establishment without parental consent and restrictions is 16.

According to a UNICEF study, it is a myth that most child labor is in sweatshops that export goods to the rich countries. Instead most children work as domestic household servants, sell products on the street, or are employed in agriculture where inspectors and journalist rarely see them.

Why is prostitution legal in some countries?

■ Prostitution is legal in the Netherlands, parts of Australia, New Zealand, Switzerland, and several other countries. In some countries (such as the UK), prostitution is not illegal, but solicitation and other activities associated with it are. In the US, prostitution is legal in some parts of Nevada. Proponents say that legalizing prostitution allows it to be regulated, protecting the safety of prostitutes and diminishing the health risks to them and their clients. It curbs sex trafficking and cuts down on violence since prosti-

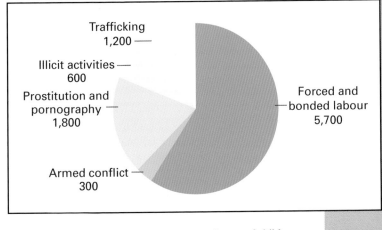

© ILO/UNICEF

Trafficking
1,200 —

Illicit activities —
600

Prostitution and
pornography —
1,800

Armed conflict —
300

Forced and
— bonded labour
5,700

**Children in unconditional worst forms of child
labor and exploitation (in thousands).**

tutes can seek legal protection. Legal prostitution is also subject to taxes and fees, representing income to the government. Prostitutes are sometimes called Commercial Sex Workers (CSWs) and some groups contend that women should have the right to choose such work as a profession.

With the spread of HIV/AIDS, some countries have made prostitution legal or chosen to recognize its existence so that health risks can be minimized. Thailand is one such country where prostitution is technically illegal but the government has chosen to acknowledge its existence in order to promote the use of condoms and HIV testing.

There is a growing international debate over whether it is better to ban prostitution and drive it underground or acknowledge it exists and regulate it. In some poor countries, children are enticed or coerced into the sex trade by being lured from the country to the city with promises of jobs. Because of the growing understanding that many prostitutes are infected with HIV, a higher price is paid for younger children, especially virgins. Sadly, this means younger and younger children are forced into prostitution.

What is human trafficking?

■ Human trafficking is the commercial trading of humans, often for purposes of prostitution, but also for slave labor. It often means taking people from poor countries, where they have little hope of economic freedom, and coercing them into situations which give them no means of escape and take away their human rights. They may end up in a foreign country or a large city and be forced to work in terrible conditions, for no pay, or in illegal industries.

In some extremely poor countries, children are sold by their parents into indentured servitude, to pay off debts, or an older child is sold to help pay for the cost of food for the younger children in the family. The parents may believe selling the child also offers him or her a chance for a better life.

What are child soldiers?

■ Child soldiers are minors who are coerced or forced into military service, often with rebel or militia groups. UNICEF defines them as anyone under the age of 18 who is part of a regular or irregular fighting force. Amnesty International estimates that there are 300 thousand child soldiers worldwide.

Most children who fall into service are kidnapped or are orphans preyed upon by "recruiters." Girls who become child soldiers are often subjected to sexual violence.

Why is illiteracy a problem?

■ According to the United Nations Educational, Scientific, and Cultural Organization (UNESCO): "Literacy is the ability to identify, understand, interpret, create, communicate, and compute, using printed and written materials associated with varying contexts. Literacy involves a continuum of learning to enable an individual to achieve his or her goals, to develop his or her knowledge and potential, and to participate fully in the wider society."

In South Asian, Arab, and Sub-Saharan African countries, illiteracy is at the highest rates, 40 to 50 percent. Most developed countries have illiteracy rates in single digits.

Illiteracy directly affects a person's ability to work at a reasonably high paying job, to exercise the rights of citizenship, to read important safety and health information, and even to be aware of impending danger.

FACT:

There are 300,000 child soldiers worldwide.

A young girl waits to be fed in a Zambian school program.

5 THE PLAYERS

Whose job is it to help the poor? Most people have some idea about various institutions but the landscape can be crowded and blurred. If there are so many organizations in the "poverty business" why isn't more being accomplished? Perhaps it is helpful to begin with an understanding of the various players and their roles.

What is the purpose of the UN? Isn't it supposed to help the world's poor?

■ The UN is an international organization with several purposes, including facilitating cooperation among countries in areas of international law, security, economic development, and equity. It was founded in 1945 by the allied powers with the purpose of preventing future wars.

The UN agencies most responsible for dealing with issues relating to poverty are the World Food Program, UNICEF (which helps children), UNAIDS (fighting the global AIDS pandemic), the World Health Organization, the High Commissioner for Refugees, and The United Nations Development Program (UNDP) which is the largest multilateral source of grant technical assistance in the world.

The UN also publishes the Human Development Index (HDI), a comparative measure ranking countries by poverty, literacy, education, life expectancy, and other factors.

Why is there so much call for reform?

■ There are various groups calling for reform of the UN for different reasons.

The UN was formed by the allied powers, and the five permanent members of the UN Security Council are the main victors of World War II. Because these nations have veto power over any UN resolution, they have much more control than other countries, a position that may not reflect their current status in the world. The countries in the Security Council are the US, the UK, Russia, China, and France. Many view this as an inadequate representation of the 192 member states and are concerned about the power they exercise with their votes.

Some think the UN administration is too bureaucratic and needs to be more transparent, accountable, and efficient. Because staffing at the UN is provided through a quota system, countries are allowed to install staff who may or may not be qualified for their position. Various US leaders have asked the UN to adopt policies which encourage the development of free markets and democracies and stop promoting policies viewed as anti-American. There are some groups that think the UN should be more involved in humanitarian issues and less involved in setting rules.

The UN Foundation was established in 1997 through a $1 billion grant from Ted Turner to help promote understanding of the UN in the US and to help support the programs of the UN, including the alleviation of poverty. It has served as a forum to promote dialogue between the US and the UN in a constructive manner.

What is the World Bank? Does it make loans to poor people?

■ The official motto of the World Bank is "Working for a world free of poverty." It is not a traditional bank and does not make personal loans or accept deposits from individuals. Instead, it provides low interest loans and grants to the world's poorest countries to improve education, health, governance, and infrastructure. It also helps countries recover from war and natural disaster by providing reconstruction assistance. The World Bank provides financial help as well as technical assistance through its 10 thousand employees who are experts in economics, health, education, agriculture, and governance. In 2005, the World Bank provided grants or loans of more than $20 billion. The institution itself is owned by 184 countries which contribute to it and guide its mission.

Why are there protests against the World Bank?

■ Over the last few years, there have been protests against the World Bank for a number of reasons. Some see it as an institution that continues to encourage indebtedness of poor countries. Some see it as a negative force in globalization. Some believe it is dominated by industrialized countries like the United States, and therefore promotes an agenda of capitalism and western values. Generally speaking, protesters believe that the global financial institu-

© Dale Hanson Bourke

Anti-globalization rioters clash with police in Edinburgh.

tions and agreements undermine local decision-making methods. Many governments and free trade institutions are seen as acting for the good of transnational (or multinational) corporations that have privileges most individuals do not have: moving freely across borders, access to natural resources, and access to large amounts of capital. They are often viewed as being insensitive to environmental damage and disrespectful of indigenous cultures. Some activists have called for an end to the legal status of corporations and the dissolution of the World Bank, IMF, and WTO.

What is the IMF?

■ The International Monetary Fund was established by international treaty in 1945 to help promote the health of the world economy. The IMF oversees the system of international payments and exchange rates that enables business to take place between countries.

The IMF's official purposes include: global financial stability, crisis management, the balanced expansion of world trade, the stability of exchange rates, the avoidance of competitive currency devaluations, and the orderly correction of a country's balance of payments problems. The 184 members of the IMF contribute to the fund based on the size of their economy and may borrow from the fund for short term needs. A country must be a member of the IMF in order to become a member of the World Bank.

What is the World Trade Organization?

■ The World Trade Organization (WTO) negotiates and oversees the rules of trade between nations. Its 150 member countries represent 97 percent of world trade and together develop, negotiate, and sign agreements by which they will operate. The goal is to help producers of goods and services, exporters, and importers conduct their business.

Isn't the WTO made up of mostly rich countries that set rules for the poorer countries?

■ Approximately three-quarters of the WTO members are developing or least developed countries. If a nation is classified as a developing country, certain provisions apply which help "level the playing field" in both trade and the implementation of the agreements.

The stated goal of the WTO is to promote free trade and stimulate economic growth. But some people argue that free trade does not help people in developing countries and only makes rich individuals and countries richer. WTO treaties have also been accused of a partial and unfair bias toward multinational corporations and wealthy nations. Protestors also claim that the issues of health, safety, and environment are typically ignored. WTO agreements also protect intellectual property rights, including the right of pharmaceutical companies to hold patents on medications. Some see this as a moral issue, since drugs that could save lives are only available to those who can afford to pay their market value.

Do the World Bank, International Monetary Fund, and WTO have anything in common?

■ Each of the three institutions has a distinct purpose and charter, but all three were formed at the end of World War II in an effort to help rebuild Europe and guard against conditions that lead to the Great

Three quarters of the World Trade Organization members are developing or least developed countries.

Depression. They are sometimes called the "Bretton Woods" institutions, named for the conference at that location in 1944 that aimed to create a new framework for the postwar global economy and lead to the creation of the IMF, the International Bank for Reconstruction and Development (IBRD), and the General Agreement on Tariffs and Trade (GATT).

As Europe recovered, the IBRD began to focus more on newly-independent countries no longer under colonial rule. It also added the International Development Association to make very low interest or no interest loans to the poorest countries. Then it added the International Finance Corporation to support private-sector investments and the Multilateral Insurance Guarantee Agency to provide insurance to corporations and individuals who invest in member countries. These institutions together now form what is known as The World Bank.

In 1994, GATT was replaced by the World Trade Organization. The WTO encompasses GATT's mandate but expands the areas of agreement and formalized the organization's status as an international, multilateral institution.

What is the World Food Program?

■ The World Food Programme (WFP) is the food aid branch of the United Nations. WFP strives to eradicate hunger and malnutrition, with the ultimate goal of eliminating the need for food aid itself.

According to its mission statement, the WFP seeks to: 1) save lives in refugee and other emergency situations; 2) improve the nutrition and quality of life of the most vulnerable people at critical times in their lives; and 3) help build assets and promote the self-reliance of poor people and communities, particularly through labor-intensive works programs.

In 2005, WFP distributed 4.2 million metric tons of food to 96.7 million people in 82 countries;

> "The issue of poverty is not a statistical issue. It is a human issue."
>
> James Wolfensohn, former president, World Bank

35 million beneficiaries were aided in emergency operations, including victims of conflict, natural disasters, and economic failure. Direct expenditures reached US$2.9 billion. WFP operations are funded by donations from world governments, corporations and private donors. In 2005 the WFP received $2.8 billion in contributions.

What was the controversy about the Oil-for-Food Program?

■ Much of the controversy surrounded the Oil-for-Food Program, established by the United Nations in 1995 and terminated in 2003, which was intended to allow Iraq to sell oil on the world market in exchange for food and other humanitarian needs for ordinary Iraqi citizens.

The program was introduced by the US in 1995, as a response to arguments that ordinary Iraqi citizens were inordinately affected by the international economic sanctions aimed at the demilitarisation of Saddam Hussein's Iraq. The sanctions were discontinued in 2003 after the United States invaded Iraq.

Food rations for sick patients in a clinic in Zambia.

The program was criticized for a number of reasons, including the belief that it actually enabled the Hussein regime to continue and put money back into Hussein's pockets through kickbacks, bribery, and other schemes. There were also allegations of misuse of funds and fraud at the highest levels of the UN. It was determined that contracts for sales of oil were awarded to those entities that would pay

FACT:

In 2005, the World Food Program distributed 4.2 million metric tons of food.

a fee back to the Iraqi government and that the program did not have adequate audits in place to guard against fraud.

What is the Global Fund?

■ Established in 2002 to increase global funding for interventions against three pandemics, The Global Fund to Fight AIDS, Tuberculosis and Malaria (its full name) is an organization which attracts funds from private and public sources and disburses funds within countries. The Global Fund is not part of the UN, but receives many services from the UN's World Health Organization and is also based in Geneva.

Significant donors to the fund include governments, foundations such as the Gates foundation, and private individuals. The Red Campaign (see photo) was an innovative retail campaign aimed at raising awareness of global health issues and providing a new source of funding for the Global Fund.

The Global Fund is a financing mechanism rather than an implementing agency, meaning that funded programs are monitored by committees in each country called Country Coordinating Mechanisms (CCMs). These local stakeholder organizations include government, NGO, UN, faith-based, and private sector partners.

The Global Fund provides initial grants based on the technical quality of applications, and provides continued funding to programs based on performance.

© The Global Fund

Bono and Oprah kick off the RED campaign to benefit the Global Fund.

> **God is in the debris of wasted opportunity and lives, and God is with us if we are with them.''**
>
> Bono

Why has there been controversy about the Global Fund?

■ Because the Global Fund does not oversee the implementation of its grants, but allows each country to manage the process, performance varies from country to country. In addition, faith-based organizations have charged that despite the percentage of work they do in some countries, they receive a disproportionately small percentage of grants. Some groups have also criticized specific programs such as those providing condoms as part of HIV/AIDS prevention.

President Bush pledged $15 billion over a five year period to HIV/AIDS, but placed most of the US funding for HIV/AIDS into PEPFAR (the President's Emergency Plan for AIDS) instead of the Global Fund to have more control over how the funds were allocated. Since that meant that a third of the US funds for prevention were designated to abstinence education, some felt that the US was short-circuiting the process which gave countries more control over their own programming. But the Bush administration felt the Global Fund had not yet demonstrated effectiveness in its process and wanted US funds to be used in countries it chose to support.

What is the G-8 and what does it have to do with alleviating poverty?

■ The G-8 is an unofficial forum of industrialized nations, including the United States, United Kingdom, Canada, France, Italy, Germany, Japan, and Russia. Together, they represent about half of the world's economy. In addition to smaller meetings held throughout the year, the G-8 leaders meet

FACT:

There are more than 2 million nonprofit organizations in the US alone.

for an annual summit to discuss the major issues affecting their countries.

In 2005, rock concert producer and activist Bob Geldof organized a series of concerts called the Live 8 to coincide with the meeting of the G-8 in Glen Eagles, Scotland. Along with Bono and the "Make Poverty History"/ONE campaign, Geldof hoped to bring attention to the problems of Africa and to urge leaders of the G-8 countries to commit to forgiving the debt owed by poor countries, increasing aid, and enacting fairer trade guidelines.

At the end of the 2005 summit, the leaders agreed to double foreign assistance by 2010, along with a series of other pledges.

In the past, G-8 summits have been targeted by activists against globalization, pollution, and other global issues.

What is the Millennium Challenge Account?

■ In 2002, President Bush called for a "new compact for global development," which links greater contributions from developed nations to greater responsibility from developing nations. The President proposed creation of the Millennium Challenge Account (MCA) in which development assistance would be provided to those countries that rule justly, invest in their people, and encourage economic freedom. Congress enacted legislation in 2004 that created the Millennium Challenge Corporation and funded its work. The MCA specifically aims to reduce poverty through economic growth, reward good policy, work with countries able to operate as partners, and focus on results.

What is the Monterrey Consensus?

■ The Monterrey Consensus is the set of agreements reached at the 2002 UN Conference on Financing for Development. New development aid commitments from the United States and the European Union and other countries were made at the conference and developing countries pledged to better governance. Countries also reached agreements on debt relief, fighting corruption, and policy coherence.

Some critics suggest that the US has ignored the consensus because the total amount of US official development assistance, while very large, is still a small percentage of the US gross domestic product and is much lower than other developed countries.

What is an "NGO"?

■ A non-governmental organization (NGO) is a non-profit group that raises at least a portion of its funding from private sources. Another term for such organizations is Private Voluntary Organization (PVO) or Private Development Organization (PDO). They may also be referred to as charities, humanitarian organizations, or relief and development agencies, depending on their purpose.

According to some estimates, there are as many as 2 million such groups in the US alone.

FACT:

In 2004 $7.1 billion was given to the developing world through private voluntary organizations (PVOs).

© Dale Hanson Bourke

The "Make Poverty History" campaign sponsored by DATA.

What is meant by relief and development? Is there a difference between them?

- In times of disaster, non-profit groups often raise funds for "relief" meaning they are providing immediate response to those in the affected region. Relief funds are typically needed in the first days and months after a disaster, such as a flood, earthquake, hurricane, or to help respond to victims of war. Some organizations consider relief funds to be those that are used in the short term. Depending on the organization, this may be from six months to two years.

Development is more long term. For example, once immediate health and safety needs are met, displaced people need more long term shelter and such services as education, job training, and ongoing health care.

Do NGOs have any set of rules by which they operate?

- There are a number of organizations that establish rules, codes of conduct, and "best practices" for NGOs. InterAction is the organization that establishes many of the ground rules for US based international humanitarian organizations. The UN, World Health Organization and other international groups also lay out guidelines and establish best practices for members.

How do we know NGOs are really helping people?

- There are a variety of ways to learn about the efficiency and effectiveness of particular nonprofit organizations. Charity Navigator is one source (www.charitynavigator.org) of information about charities and provides basic information about the organizations and certain aspects of their finances.

Any charity must also provide access to their financial statements, including their form 990. An educated donor will take the time to review the information in this document, including the pay of the top executives and the areas where dollars are being spent.

Besides the accountability an organization owes private individuals, NGOs must also report to government and foundation donors.

What are foundations?

■ A foundation is a legal entity set up to distribute grants. Some of the largest foundations are the Gates Foundation and the Ford Foundation. There are also thousands of family foundations, created to distribute the wealth of a family or individual.

© Amy Turner, World Vision

A young girl drinks water from a pump provided by World Vision to help the displaced during a time of conflict within Liberia.

What are faith-based organizations? What type of work do they do?

- Faith-based organizations do almost every type of humanitarian work but are generally operated along the principles or tenets of a particular religion or faith. Most prefer to hire individuals who agree with the values of the organization but do not necessarily serve only those who subscribe to the same beliefs.

The Salvation Army, World Vision, and Catholic Charities are some of the largest faith-based organizations.

Does the government fund proselytizing?

- No. Public money given to faith-based organizations must be used for humanitarian or other assistance and the work must be kept separate from any proselytizing, worship services, or other types of religious work done by the organization.

What was Jubilee 2000?

- During the late 1990s, a citizen's campaign took hold in churches and among those concerned about Africa to make 2000 a "year of jubilee" for poor nations struggling with excessive external debt. The name came from the Old Testament concept of a jubilee year being a time when all debt was cancelled.

The campaign raised awareness of the fact that many African nations were enormously indebted to rich governments and international institutions which had loaned money to often corrupt leaders in the 1980s and 1990s. The loans accrued enormous interest and some countries could barely keep up with the interest payments, let alone repay capital.

> " **Poor health is both a cause of poverty and a consequence of poverty.** "
>
> Dr. Helene Gayle, president of CARE

As a result, nations could not invest in national education, health, or infrastructure and still meet the debt burden.

Do public institutions and private groups work together?

■ Increasingly, public and private partnerships are forming to fight specific problems and offer leveraged responses. Examples include The Global Fund, The Global Alliance for Vaccines and Immunization (GAVI) which aims to vaccinate children worldwide, and Malaria No More, which was formed to prevent and treat malaria in poor countries.

What is the Human Development Index?

■ The UN Human Development Index (HDI) is a comparative measure of poverty, literacy, education, life expectancy, childbirth, and other factors for countries worldwide. It is a standard means of measuring well-being and is used by many people to distinguish whether or not the country is a first, second, or third world country.

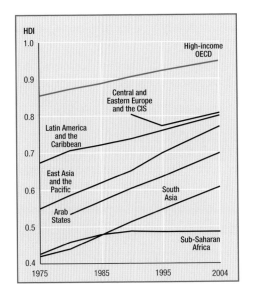

The human development trend by area

Homeless in America.

6 US POVERTY

How can we talk about global poverty without looking at the poor closest to us? It's an issue that is debated by politicians, economists and theologians and one of the more divisive issues in the broader topic of poverty. On one hand, a poor person in the US is still unimaginably wealthier than a poor person in a developing country. On the other hand, the US is by far the wealthiest country on earth and still has the highest poverty rate among highly developed countries. Poverty in the US is complex. Here are just some of the questions people have about it.

Why should we be so concerned about the rest of the world when people are poor in the US?

■ It is true that a significant percentage of Americans are poor. But people who are considered poor in the US are rarely starving, dying of thirst, or remain untreated from simple diseases, like people in developing countries. The US offers emergency medical care to anyone who needs it and food banks, emergency shelters, and other public and private resources are available to the poor in this country, in contrast to those in the developing world.

On the other hand, the US is by far the richest country in the world and the level of poverty in this country is surprising to some and an outrage to many. So we need to help both groups.

What does it mean to be poor in America?

■ Poverty in America is different from poverty in the developing world for a variety of reasons. Poverty is defined as having a family income that is less than the poverty line. In 2007 that means that a family of four living on less than $20,650 is living below the poverty line and is, therefore, considered "poor." An individual who makes less than $10,210 is poor, but that is equal to living on $28 per day.

Unlike the poor in developing countries, a person who is poor in the US often has adequate food, clothing, and shelter. More than 70 percent of the poor own cars and 46 percent own homes. Poverty in the US is often a temporary condition, so a family may fall below the poverty line one year, but will often recover the next. Although 13 percent of the population of the US is currently below the poverty line, those who make up that number will change from year to year.

Some economists suggest that in a developed country, poverty should be defined as "significantly less access to income and wealth than other members of society." By that definition the poverty rate is linked to income inequality.

Who sets the poverty line?

■ The US government sets the poverty line each year at approximately three times the annual cost of a nutritional meal. This measure was developed in the 1960s as part of the "War on Poverty" program and has been increasingly controversial because it is an absolute measure, meaning it doesn't change depending on other factors. It is adjusted annually to reflect changes in the consumer price index.

Isn't it harder to live on that amount in a major city than in a rural area?

■ Yes, one of the criticisms of the poverty line is that it is the same for all 48 contiguous states and the District of Columbia. (Hawaii and Alaska have higher rates.) It does not account for such variables as the cost of fuel in cold regions, the higher cost of living in a city like New York, the inadequate public transportation systems in some regions, and the high cost of housing in some cities.

Couldn't poor people just get a job?

■ Many of those who are considered poor in the US are the "working poor." They have jobs, but earn too little to adequately cover their needs. Some work at temporary or seasonal jobs or lack job security. And many elderly or disabled people cannot work because of physical problems.

One of the reasons people cite for raising the minimum wage is that a person working at a job that pays the minimum wage cannot support a family without falling below the poverty line. A single mother cannot afford childcare while working at the minimum wage. Even a single person without dependents cannot qualify for housing in some cases if she earns the minimum wage.

What is the minimum wage and how does it get set?

■ The minimum wage is the lowest rate an employee can be legally paid by an employer. Most countries have a minimum wage, although some countries do not have minimum wages set by the government but rather rely on unions and other groups to set wages. In the US, the minimum wage is set by Congress but can be vetoed by the president. Under President Clinton, states were given the power to set their own minimum wage. More than half the states had done so at the beginning of 2007, and even some counties and cities had set higher rates.

Some politicians suggest that the minimum wage should be linked to the Consumer Price Index. Some economists believe the minimum wage is a deterrent to economic growth and actually harms the poorest workers because it increases unemployment at the low end of the labor pool.

Why do some poor workers get big tax checks from the government?

■ Some of the working poor qualify for the Earned Income Tax Credit or EITC. To receive this benefit, a person has to be working and file a tax return with the IRS. For the most part, any taxes paid are refunded and in some cases, a subsidy is paid. Because this program benefits workers making as much as $36,000 per year (depending on the size of the family) it benefits a broad spectrum of people working at low wage jobs. Since welfare reform in 1996, the EITC has become the primary anti-poverty program in the US.

Many politicians and economists praise this program because it encourages people to work and to document their earnings. Workers who are not citizens are sometimes reluctant to do so, for fear of having their immigration status questioned.

What is welfare? Does it still exist?

■ Welfare is government funding or assistance given to the poor—usually families with children. Since the welfare reform act in 1996, individual are limited to a lifetime maximum of five years for receiving federal welfare of any type. In addition, what was known as Aid to Families with Dependent Children (AFDC) was replaced by Temporary Assistance for Needy Families (TANF), which includes more limits on the amount of time an individual or family can receive welfare. Part of the same act created the Earned Income Tax Credit (EITC) although most do not consider it welfare, but rather a way to help the working poor. Unemployment compensation is another way the government offers assistance to those who might otherwise fall into poverty, although it is not considered welfare per se.

Do poor people still get food stamps?

■ Yes, food stamps are a form of federal assistance to alleviate poverty in the US. Benefits are distributed by states, but the program is administered through the U.S. Department of Agriculture. Food stamps used to be paper coupons but most food stamp benefits are now distributed using Electronic Benefit Transfer (EBT) cards.

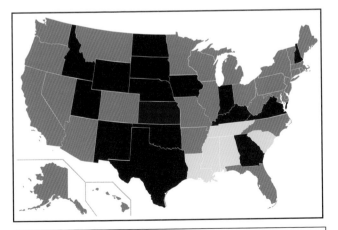

Minimum Wage by State

States with minimum wage rates higher than the Federal minimum wage
States with minimum wage rates equal to the Federal minimum wage
States with no minimum wage law
States with minimum wage rates lower than the Federal minimum wage

US Poverty

According to the US Department of Agriculture, 79 percent of all benefits go to households with children, 16 percent go to households with disabled persons, and 7 percent go to households with elderly persons. The average gross monthly income per food stamp household is $640. The ethnic makeup of food stamp recipients are: 41 percent white; 36 percent African-American, non-Hispanic; 18 percent Hispanic; 3 percent Asian, 2 percent Native American, and 1 percent are of unknown race or ethnicity.

Are some groups of people more inclined to be poor?

■ Poverty cuts across all ages and ethnic groups. The largest percentage of poor are white. While African Americans are overrepresented, they tend to make up about one quarter of those considered poor. Immigrants who do not have legal status tend to be quite poor, mostly because they work at very low paying jobs and lack language skills. But because they are often undocumented it is difficult to measure their plight accurately.

Are more people poor now than before?

■ The official percentage of people living in poverty in the US has remained relatively stable for many years. Some say the way the poverty line is established is flawed so it doesn't accurately reflect a rising number of

2007 Department of Health and Human Services Poverty Guidelines

Persons in Family	48 Contiguous States and D.C.	Alaska	Hawaii
1	$10,210	$12,770	$11,750
2	13,690	17,120	15,750
3	17,170	21,470	19,750
4	20,650	25,820	23,750
5	24,130	30,170	27,750
6	27,610	34,520	31,750
7	31,090	38,870	35,750
8	34,570	43,220	39,750
For each additional person, add	3,480	4,350	4,000

people—especially elderly and working poor—who are barely making ends meet. Others point to the high number of immigrants who are poor but are not officially measured in the statistics.

How does the US compare to other developed countries when it comes to dealing with poor citizens?

■ In Europe, the EU defines poverty as an income below 60 percent of the national median, after social transfers. This means that a higher number of the population is considered poor, but if that measure was used in the US, our poverty rate would rise from 13 percent to 24 percent. When poverty measures are comparable, the US has one of the highest rates of poverty in the developed world.

What is meant by "the feminization of poverty"?

■ Women account for more than half of those considered poor in the US, and have been the majority of the poor since the 1970s. Although the total rate has not significantly increased, the sense that women account for an increasing number of poor people has led many people to talk about poverty in the US as the feminization of poverty, especially since such a high percentage of the poor live in female-headed households.

Women tend to have higher poverty rates than men because they have fewer economic resources, and because they are more often single parents and must pay for childcare. Children do not contribute to income but do add expenses, and women must often choose a less demanding job so that they can be home in the evenings to care for their children.

Through a grant provided by **USAID**, this woman prepares to
visit **AIDS** patients in their homes.

7 WHAT WORKS

Conquering poverty is an enormous challenge but it is not insurmountable. Many organizations are working to alleviate hunger, reduce infant mortality, limit the effects of drought and provide sustainable development solutions. But they need help. Investing in solutions to poverty can mean donating to an organization or advocating on behalf of the poor. This chapter discusses some ways to get involved, be informed, and take the first steps toward making a difference. At the end of this chapter is a list of websites and books to learn even more.

I am a donor to a humanitarian organization and sometimes wonder if my contribution really makes a difference. How can I know?

■ Giving to a nonprofit organization should be a way to not only help others but also to become educated about the issues. Start by reading the website of the organization to see how they operate and exactly what type of work they do. Does the organization do the work itself or pass the contributions through to others? Is the organization accredited by one of the watchdog agencies? Charity Navigator (www.charitynavigator.com) is one way to get basic information about a nonprofit organization and an overview of their work and efficiency.

If you are a donor you have the right to ask for more information about the work and should request an annual report. You may also want to review the form 990, a detailed financial report every nonprofit must file and must make available to anyone who requests a copy. Most organizations have a copy available on their website. The 990 shows exactly how much of the organization's funds went to work in different areas and also lists the salaries of the top executives.

What ways can a person help besides giving money?

■ Many nonprofits offer ways for citizen involvement, including letter writing campaigns to members of Congress, opportunities to raise awareness and funds through walk-a-thons or other public events, and even buttons or bumper stickers to use to raise awareness of issues. Some organizations believe that public advocacy for a cause is as important as the donations they receive.

The ONE campaign (www.data.org) has mobilized citizens on issues surrounding debt, trade and Africa. Bread for the World (www.breadfortheworld.org) helps mobilize congregations around hunger policies. More and more nonprofits offer e-mail alerts to help educate their supporters about pending legislation.

What is advocacy? Does it really make a difference?

■ Advocacy simply means lending your voice to a cause as a private citizen. Although some organizations actually hire lobbyists to represent them to lawmakers, most believe that a public response to an issue creates an even greater sense of urgency. Citizens who march, write letters to their representative or newspaper, display bumper stickers, or in other ways advocate for an issue are becoming an increasingly important force in policy-making.

> " When I give food to the poor they call me a saint. When I ask why the poor have no food they call me a communist."
>
> Helder Camara

How can I get educated about the facts?

- Organizations such as the Center for Global Development (www.cgdev.org) are committed to education about broad and specific issues affecting the poor. There are also groups committed to education about specific areas, such as malaria (www.malarianomore.org) and hunger (www.bread.org). A longer list of websites appears at the back of this book. There are also organizations like the World Bank which sponsors a site just about poverty issues (www.povertynet.org) and the UN, which has sites on children, refugees, AIDS, and other specific concerns.

FACT:

Protestant missions gave $4.5 billion to international causes in 2003.

© Dale Hanson Bourke

Freshly-dug graves in Lusaka, Zambia, provide a vivid reminder that death is common in poor African countries.

My church is taking a trip to Africa to do missions work. Some people think we should save our money from the ticket and donate that instead of going. How can we know what is most effective?

■ As churches and synagogues have become more active in so-called mission trips, many have raised the question about using the money more effectively by sending it to help rather than using it on travel expenses.

Going to actually see the needs of the world is a very valuable experience. There really is no substitute for spending time with people, developing relationships, and beginning to see, first hand, the reality of life in poor countries. In some ways, the understanding that comes from such a trip may be more important than any work that is accomplished. Until a person experiences the reality of poverty and understands the difficulty of accomplishing even simple things in a poor culture, it is hard to truly empathize with the poor.

One way some faith communities are accomplishing both is by sending a small, representative group to a project and including a video-grapher and writer to help record the experiences. That way more members of the community can share in the learnings without spending so much on travel.

Is it better to support a small organization or a larger one?

■ Large organizations typically have the ability to respond more quickly, be more efficient, and have greater capacity. Small organizations may have higher overhead because they lack economies of scale but they are also often more focused on a particular need or one type of response instead of responding to many different issues. Sometimes a donor feels more important to a small organization and likes the sense of responsiveness. Others like being part of a large organization and a big movement and giving to a cause that is well known to the public.

How can we encourage groups to work together and not duplicate efforts?

■ Increasingly, organizations are working together or voluntarily cooperating in efforts to develop a framework for the work. There are groups in each country trying to become a clearinghouse for non-profits, as well as organizations dedicated to certain type of work, such as HIV/AIDS assistance, water projects, and immunizations. The UN is generally the coordinating agency in times of disaster,

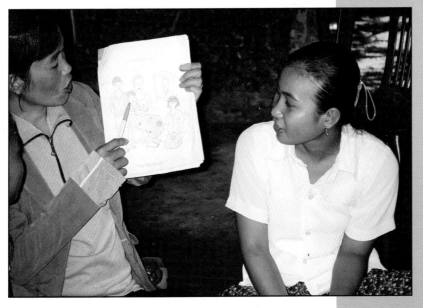

© Dale Hanson Bourke

Health education helps women care for themselves and their families.

helping aid flow quickly and efficiently to those who need help.

Is child sponsorship a good way to help children?

▪ Child sponsorship exists primarily as a way to help people in developed countries identify with one poor child. Groups like World Vision, Save the Children, Compassion, and others have used child sponsorship as a development model for many years. It has been a very powerful tool for keeping donors engaged and for educating donors about the types of issues facing that child. Over the years, most child sponsorship organizations have grown from helping just the individual child to creating infrastructure to assist the entire community.

The largest child sponsorship organizations voluntarily cooperate with one another to promote best practices and to minimize potential harm to the children. This includes making sure donations actually go to the intended purpose, and keeping donors from visiting children without notice, since this has created some instances of child predators gaining access to children.

> **A key solution to suffering lies in providing a voice for the poor—in providing hands on advocacy that brings the rule of law back to poor communities."**
>
> Gary A. Haugen, President of International Justice Mission

Through child sponsorship, items such as this container to hold clean water are provided to those in need.

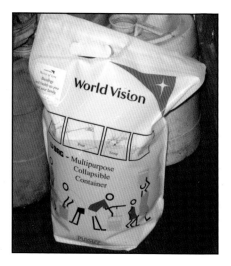

© Dale Hanson Bourke

Organizations based on a child sponsorship model keep children as the focus of their work. As with any organization, it is important to check that a particular group is accredited or review the documents from the organization so that you feel good about your donation.

What is microfinance and how does it help people?

■ Microfinance has become one of the most effective ways to help the poor move up and out of poverty. Muhammad Yunus won the Nobel Peace Prize in 2006 for his work in microfinance through the Grameen Bank, which operates in Bangladesh. Microfinance entails making small loans without collateral to poor people. Usually there is some training or advice that goes along with the loan to help a poor person learn how to improve his or her business.

There are a number of microfinance organizations, some faith-based or with a particular emphasis to their work. Many emphasize group loans, meaning a group of individuals comes together to cross-collateralize the loans. Most organizations give the majority of their loans to women.

An increasing emphasis is on providing savings opportunities for the poor. Traditionally, the poor could not safely accumulate funds, so had a hard time saving enough to pay for schooling or to buy property. As the poor are able to create income

Less than 10 percent of Americans have current passports.

Members of a microfinance group in Honduras review their small loans.

because of loans, they also need to be able to save money in banks, where it will gain interest and remain secure.

Other financial products growing out of microfinance include insurance for health, burial costs (important in areas where deaths from AIDS is significant), crop failure, and other natural disasters.

How does one person get started?

■ Reading this book and then finding more information on websites or through the bibliography (page 109) is a good way to start. Are there certain types of poverty-related problems that particularly interest you? Learning more about the causes of those particular problems may lead you to an organization already working to solve the problem. Do you wish others knew more about the problems of poverty? Why not organize a group at your office, place of worship, or school to study the issues and suggest ways to get involved?

Some organizations, like DATA (www.data.org) or Bread for the World (www.bread.org) are particularly helpful in providing information to use with

A group of American women visit a project in the Dominican Republic as part of a mission trip.

friends or to share with your church, synagogue, or mosque. The Center for Global Development (www.cgdev.org) offers studies and open forums on issues relating to poverty. Some groups sponsor public campaigns and need local organizers. Others have particular days designated for activism.

There are numbers of ways for a person to get involved and more than ever, there is evidence that one person does make a difference.

If I want to help make a difference in the world, should I major in any particular subject in college?

■ Some students know what they want to do and go to college in order to study international relations or to major in subjects directly related to global poverty. Others major in economics or business and make their way into a field like microfinance. People working for nonprofits or humanitarian organizations often come from many backgrounds, including health, communications, sociology, or psychology.

Perhaps the best way to know what area is of interest is to spend a summer working as an intern with a nonprofit and learn more about the particular area that might be of interest. Or look at the website for the Peace Corps (www.peacecorps.gov) and find out what areas interest you. You may also discover that your denomination or faith group has summer service opportunities.

Is there any way to make a difference during a brief vacation or spring break?

■ Yes. More and more organizations are providing short-term opportunities for students. Check your school's student activity website for such oppor-

FACT:

One of the Millennium Development Goals aims to reduce mortality among children under five by two-thirds.

tunities. One of the most popular projects is to go to a Habitat for Humanity site and, together with your friends, help construct housing for the poor. (www.habitat.org)

Does it make a difference if I write or call my Senator or Representative?

■ Yes. Writing to your Members of Congress is one of the most important things you can do. They rely on your voice to tell them what issues are of interest to their constituents.

The first step is to know who represents your district. You can go to www.congress.org and look up your representative by zip code. You can also search the issues that interest you and find out who sits on key committees.

You can also call the office of your Senator or Representative. Call (202) 224-3121 and ask for the office. You will probably get an aide who will be happy to take a brief message about an issue or pending legislation.

What about writing a letter to the editor? Do they ever get read?

■ Letters to the editor do get read and often get published, so be sure you write something that you are willing to have appear in a subsequent issue. Support your position with facts and try to stay away from emotional or caustic comments. If you feel an issue has not been covered recently, explain why you think the publication should include it.

For example, if you are confused about an issue like immigration or the role of the UN, ask the editor to consider including more articles that give you a

"

The poor person has to exist so he can serve the great one, the rich. God made things like that."

A poor man in Brazil (*Voice of the Poor*)

basic overview so you can more fully appreciate the significance of news events.

While some organizations send out form letters and ask people to send them to publications or Members of Congress, a personal letter is always more effective than a form letter.

Have organizations agreed to work together on specific goals?

■ The Millenium Development Goals were adopted in 2000 and have specific targets to accomplish by 2015. Many organizations have framed their own programs in terms of these goals and there is a website that updates the progress toward the goals: http://www.un.org/millenniumgoals.

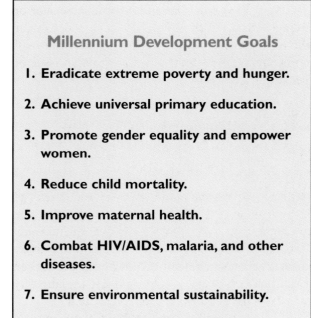

Millennium Development Goals

1. **Eradicate extreme poverty and hunger.**

2. **Achieve universal primary education.**

3. **Promote gender equality and empower women.**

4. **Reduce child mortality.**

5. **Improve maternal health.**

6. **Combat HIV/AIDS, malaria, and other diseases.**

7. **Ensure environmental sustainability.**

8. **Develop a global partnership for development.**

FACT:

More than $4.5 billion was given online in 2005.

What makes these goals especially meaningful is that they address ways that all organizations can work toward specific and agreed upon causes of poverty. Their methods may vary, but almost all groups agree that the MDGs are worthy goals.

What is the most important thing to do?

■ The most important thing is to do something. Read about the issue. Tell someone else. Write a letter. Give a donation. Start a book group. Teach a Sunday school class. Pray. Go to a website. Visit a poor country. Visit a poor neighborhood in your town. Give something you no longer use to a charity. Volunteer in a soup kitchen. Tutor a child.

American Carrie Slease meets school children while on a mission trip to Uganda with Opportunity International.

© Dale Hanson Rourke

Selected Bibliography

Africa: A Biography of the Continent. John Reader. Vintage Books, 1999.

African Development: Making Sense of the Issues and Actors. Todd Moss. Lynne Reinner Publishers Inc., 2007.

Banker to the Poor. Muhammad Yunnus. Public Affairs, 2003.

The Bible. New International Version. International Bible Society/Zondervan,

Culture and Prosperity. John Kay. Harper Business, 2004.

"The Challenge of Global Health." Laurie Garrett. *Foreign Affairs*, January/February 2007, pg. 14

The End of Poverty. Jeffrey D. Sachs. Penguin, 2005.

Ending Global Poverty. Stephen C. Smith. Palgrave Macmillan, 2005.

The Extreme Future. James Canton. Dutton, 2006.

"From Poverty to Prosperity." Center for American Progress, 2007.

Give Us Your Best and Brightest. Devesh Kapur and John McHale. Center for Global Development, 2005.

God of the Empty-Handed. Jayakumar Christian. MARC, 1999.

God's Politics. Jim Wallis. Harper San Francisco, 2005.

"Helping People Help Themselves." Teresa Tritch. *The New York Times*, Feb. 14, 2007.

Human Development Report 2006. United Nations Development Programme. Palgrave Macmillan, 2006.

Introducing Global Issues. Michael T. Snarr and D. Neil Snarr. Rienner, 2005.

King Leopold's Ghost. Adam Hochschild. Mariner Books, 1999.

Let Their People Come. Lant Pritchett. Center for Global Development, 2006.

Making Globalization Work. Joseph E. Stiglitz. Norton, 2006.

MiniAtlas of Millenium Development Goals. The World Bank. Myriad Editions/The World Bank, 2005.

The Mystery of Capital. Hernando de Soto. Basic Books, 2000.

The Other America. Michael Harrington. Simon & Schuster, 1993.

The Other Path. Hernando de Soto. Basic Books, 1989.

Poverty in America. John Iceland. University of California Press, 2006.

Rich Christians in an Age of Hunger. Ronald J. Sider. Word, 1997.

The State of the World's Children 2006. UNICEF. UNICEF, 2005.

Understanding Poverty. Edited by Abhijit Vinayak Banerjee, Roland Benabou and Dilip Mookherjee. Oxford University Press, 2006.

US in the World. Rockefeller Brothers Fund and The Aspen Institute, 2004.

Vital Signs 2006–2007. Worldwatch Institute. Norton/Worldwatch, 2006.

Voices of the Poor: Can Anyone Hear Us? Deepa Narayan. Oxford University Press/World Bank, 2000.

Voices of the Poor: From Many Lands. Deepa Narayan and Patti Petesch. Oxford University Press/World Bank, 2002.

The White Man's Burden. William Easterly. Penguin, 2006.

The Working Poor. David K. Shipler. Vintage, 2005.

World Bank Atlas. The World Bank, 2004.

Recommended Websites

www.bread.org	Bread for the World
www.census.org	Statistics on US population, including poverty.
www.cgdev.org	The Center for Global Development is an independent think tank that works to reduce global poverty and inequality through rigorous research and active engagement with the policy community.
www.charitynavigator.org	Charity Navigator gives information on various charities.
www.ecfa.org	Lists members of the Evangelical Council on Financial Accountability.
www.theglobalfund.org	Official site of the Global Fund for AIDS, Malaria and Tuberculosis
www.idealist.org	Offers opportunities for volunteer and paid positions.
www.interaction.org	InterAction is the association of US based international relief and development agencies.
www.one.org	The One Campaign
www.servenet.org	Offers volunteer positions in the US.
www.unicef.org	The United Nations Children's Fund.
www.usaid.gov	The US Agency for International Development.
www.who.org	World Health Organization.
www.worldbank.org	The World Bank

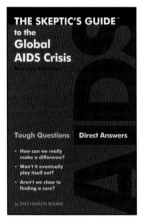